C-4210   CAREER EXAMINATION SERIES

This is your
PASSBOOK for...

Plant Maintainer

Test Preparation Study Guide
Questions & Answers

COPYRIGHT NOTICE

This book is SOLELY intended for, is sold ONLY to, and its use is RESTRICTED to individual, bona fide applicants or candidates who qualify by virtue of having seriously filed applications for appropriate license, certificate, professional and/or promotional advancement, higher school matriculation, scholarship, or other legitimate requirements of education and/or governmental authorities.

This book is NOT intended for use, class instruction, tutoring, training, duplication, copying, reprinting, excerption, or adaptation, etc., by:

1) Other publishers
2) Proprietors and/or Instructors of "Coaching" and/or Preparatory Courses
3) Personnel and/or Training Divisions of commercial, industrial, and governmental organizations
4) Schools, colleges, or universities and/or their departments and staffs, including teachers and other personnel
5) Testing Agencies or Bureaus
6) Study groups which seek by the purchase of a single volume to copy and/or duplicate and/or adapt this material for use by the group as a whole without having purchased individual volumes for each of the members of the group
7) Et al.

Such persons would be in violation of appropriate Federal and State statutes.

PROVISION OF LICENSING AGREEMENTS – Recognized educational, commercial, industrial, and governmental institutions and organizations, and others legitimately engaged in educational pursuits, including training, testing, and measurement activities, may address request for a licensing agreement to the copyright owners, who will determine whether, and under what conditions, including fees and charges, the materials in this book may be used them. In other words, a licensing facility exists for the legitimate use of the material in this book on other than an individual basis. However, it is asseverated and affirmed here that the material in this book CANNOT be used without the receipt of the express permission of such a licensing agreement from the Publishers. Inquiries re licensing should be addressed to the company, attention rights and permissions department.

All rights reserved, including the right of reproduction in whole or in part, in any form or by any means, electronic or mechanical, including photocopying, recording, or by any information storage and retrieval system, without permission in writing from the Publisher.

Copyright © 2025 by
National Learning Corporation

212 Michael Drive, Syosset, NY 11791
(516) 921-8888 • www.passbooks.com
E-mail: info@passbooks.com

PASSBOOK® SERIES

THE *PASSBOOK® SERIES* has been created to prepare applicants and candidates for the ultimate academic battlefield – the examination room.

At some time in our lives, each and every one of us may be required to take an examination – for validation, matriculation, admission, qualification, registration, certification, or licensure.

Based on the assumption that every applicant or candidate has met the basic formal educational standards, has taken the required number of courses, and read the necessary texts, the *PASSBOOK® SERIES* furnishes the one special preparation which may assure passing with confidence, instead of failing with insecurity. Examination questions – together with answers – are furnished as the basic vehicle for study so that the mysteries of the examination and its compounding difficulties may be eliminated or diminished by a sure method.

This book is meant to help you pass your examination provided that you qualify and are serious in your objective.

The entire field is reviewed through the huge store of content information which is succinctly presented through a provocative and challenging approach – the question-and-answer method.

A climate of success is established by furnishing the correct answers at the end of each test.

You soon learn to recognize types of questions, forms of questions, and patterns of questioning. You may even begin to anticipate expected outcomes.

You perceive that many questions are repeated or adapted so that you can gain acute insights, which may enable you to score many sure points.

You learn how to confront new questions, or types of questions, and to attack them confidently and work out the correct answers.

You note objectives and emphases, and recognize pitfalls and dangers, so that you may make positive educational adjustments.

Moreover, you are kept fully informed in relation to new concepts, methods, practices, and directions in the field.

You discover that you are actually taking the examination all the time: you are preparing for the examination by "taking" an examination, not by reading extraneous and/or supererogatory textbooks.

In short, this PASSBOOK®, used directedly, should be an important factor in helping you to pass your test.

PLANT MAINTAINER

WHAT THE JOB INVOLVES:

Plant Maintainers, under supervision, install, lubricate, maintain and tend power plant, pumping, heating, ventilating, refrigeration, air conditioning equipment and related systems serving hospitals and health care facilities; inspect, maintain, repair and/or tend equipment used in heating, ventilating, refrigeration, air conditioning and related mechanical systems; inspect and read meters, gauges and other controls of operating equipment may tend and/or boilers and incinerator furnaces and related equipment; except that where equipment requires a high pressure boiler or refrigeration mechanic operator's license, may assist in this function; may, if necessary, in selected institutions, hand fire high pressure boilers using solid fuels; clean burners; may dismantle and/or assemble equipment associated with the heating, ventilating, refrigeration, air conditioning or mechanical systems and make operational; may requisition parts as required; and maintain necessary work records and logs; perform related work.

The multiple-choice test may include questions on the operation and maintenance of high pressure boilers including burner, ignition, controls, valves, pumps, meters, gauges and regulators; operation and maintenance of auxiliaries and refrigeration equipment; selection and usage of lubricants, packing and gaskets; use of appropriate tools, instruments and lubricating devices; safety; number facility; written comprehension; written expression; and other related areas.

HOW TO TAKE A TEST

I. YOU MUST PASS AN EXAMINATION

A. *WHAT EVERY CANDIDATE SHOULD KNOW*

Examination applicants often ask us for help in preparing for the written test. What can I study in advance? What kinds of questions will be asked? How will the test be given? How will the papers be graded?

As an applicant for a civil service examination, you may be wondering about some of these things. Our purpose here is to suggest effective methods of advance study and to describe civil service examinations.

Your chances for success on this examination can be increased if you know how to prepare. Those "pre-examination jitters" can be reduced if you know what to expect. You can even experience an adventure in good citizenship if you know why civil service exams are given.

B. *WHY ARE CIVIL SERVICE EXAMINATIONS GIVEN?*

Civil service examinations are important to you in two ways. As a citizen, you want public jobs filled by employees who know how to do their work. As a job seeker, you want a fair chance to compete for that job on an equal footing with other candidates. The best-known means of accomplishing this two-fold goal is the competitive examination.

Exams are widely publicized throughout the nation. They may be administered for jobs in federal, state, city, municipal, town or village governments or agencies.

Any citizen may apply, with some limitations, such as the age or residence of applicants. Your experience and education may be reviewed to see whether you meet the requirements for the particular examination. When these requirements exist, they are reasonable and applied consistently to all applicants. Thus, a competitive examination may cause you some uneasiness now, but it is your privilege and safeguard.

C. *HOW ARE CIVIL SERVICE EXAMS DEVELOPED?*

Examinations are carefully written by trained technicians who are specialists in the field known as "psychological measurement," in consultation with recognized authorities in the field of work that the test will cover. These experts recommend the subject matter areas or skills to be tested; only those knowledges or skills important to your success on the job are included. The most reliable books and source materials available are used as references. Together, the experts and technicians judge the difficulty level of the questions.

Test technicians know how to phrase questions so that the problem is clearly stated. Their ethics do not permit "trick" or "catch" questions. Questions may have been tried out on sample groups, or subjected to statistical analysis, to determine their usefulness.

Written tests are often used in combination with performance tests, ratings of training and experience, and oral interviews. All of these measures combine to form the best-known means of finding the right person for the right job.

II. HOW TO PASS THE WRITTEN TEST

A. NATURE OF THE EXAMINATION

To prepare intelligently for civil service examinations, you should know how they differ from school examinations you have taken. In school you were assigned certain definite pages to read or subjects to cover. The examination questions were quite detailed and usually emphasized memory. Civil service exams, on the other hand, try to discover your present ability to perform the duties of a position, plus your potentiality to learn these duties. In other words, a civil service exam attempts to predict how successful you will be. Questions cover such a broad area that they cannot be as minute and detailed as school exam questions.

In the public service similar kinds of work, or positions, are grouped together in one "class." This process is known as *position-classification*. All the positions in a class are paid according to the salary range for that class. One class title covers all of these positions, and they are all tested by the same examination.

B. FOUR BASIC STEPS

1) Study the announcement

How, then, can you know what subjects to study? Our best answer is: "Learn as much as possible about the class of positions for which you've applied." The exam will test the knowledge, skills and abilities needed to do the work.

Your most valuable source of information about the position you want is the official exam announcement. This announcement lists the training and experience qualifications. Check these standards and apply only if you come reasonably close to meeting them.

The brief description of the position in the examination announcement offers some clues to the subjects which will be tested. Think about the job itself. Review the duties in your mind. Can you perform them, or are there some in which you are rusty? Fill in the blank spots in your preparation.

Many jurisdictions preview the written test in the exam announcement by including a section called "Knowledge and Abilities Required," "Scope of the Examination," or some similar heading. Here you will find out specifically what fields will be tested.

2) Review your own background

Once you learn in general what the position is all about, and what you need to know to do the work, ask yourself which subjects you already know fairly well and which need improvement. You may wonder whether to concentrate on improving your strong areas or on building some background in your fields of weakness. When the announcement has specified "some knowledge" or "considerable knowledge," or has used adjectives like "beginning principles of..." or "advanced ... methods," you can get a clue as to the number and difficulty of questions to be asked in any given field. More questions, and hence broader coverage, would be included for those subjects which are more important in the work. Now weigh your strengths and weaknesses against the job requirements and prepare accordingly.

3) Determine the level of the position

Another way to tell how intensively you should prepare is to understand the level of the job for which you are applying. Is it the entering level? In other words, is this the position in which beginners in a field of work are hired? Or is it an intermediate or advanced level? Sometimes this is indicated by such words as "Junior" or "Senior" in the class title. Other jurisdictions use Roman numerals to designate the level – Clerk I, Clerk II, for example. The word "Supervisor" sometimes appears in the title. If the level is not indicated by the title, check the description of duties. Will you be working under very close supervision, or will you have responsibility for independent decisions in this work?

4) Choose appropriate study materials

Now that you know the subjects to be examined and the relative amount of each subject to be covered, you can choose suitable study materials. For beginning level jobs, or even advanced ones, if you have a pronounced weakness in some aspect of your training, read a modern, standard textbook in that field. Be sure it is up to date and has general coverage. Such books are normally available at your library, and the librarian will be glad to help you locate one. For entry-level positions, questions of appropriate difficulty are chosen – neither highly advanced questions, nor those too simple. Such questions require careful thought but not advanced training.

If the position for which you are applying is technical or advanced, you will read more advanced, specialized material. If you are already familiar with the basic principles of your field, elementary textbooks would waste your time. Concentrate on advanced textbooks and technical periodicals. Think through the concepts and review difficult problems in your field.

These are all general sources. You can get more ideas on your own initiative, following these leads. For example, training manuals and publications of the government agency which employs workers in your field can be useful, particularly for technical and professional positions. A letter or visit to the government department involved may result in more specific study suggestions, and certainly will provide you with a more definite idea of the exact nature of the position you are seeking.

III. KINDS OF TESTS

Tests are used for purposes other than measuring knowledge and ability to perform specified duties. For some positions, it is equally important to test ability to make adjustments to new situations or to profit from training. In others, basic mental abilities not dependent on information are essential. Questions which test these things may not appear as pertinent to the duties of the position as those which test for knowledge and information. Yet they are often highly important parts of a fair examination. For very general questions, it is almost impossible to help you direct your study efforts. What we can do is to point out some of the more common of these general abilities needed in public service positions and describe some typical questions.

1) General information

Broad, general information has been found useful for predicting job success in some kinds of work. This is tested in a variety of ways, from vocabulary lists to questions about current events. Basic background in some field of work, such as sociology or economics, may be sampled in a group of questions. Often these are principles which have become familiar to most persons through exposure rather than through formal training. It is difficult to advise you how to study for these questions; being alert to the world around you is our best suggestion.

2) Verbal ability

An example of an ability needed in many positions is verbal or language ability. Verbal ability is, in brief, the ability to use and understand words. Vocabulary and grammar tests are typical measures of this ability. Reading comprehension or paragraph interpretation questions are common in many kinds of civil service tests. You are given a paragraph of written material and asked to find its central meaning.

3) Numerical ability

Number skills can be tested by the familiar arithmetic problem, by checking paired lists of numbers to see which are alike and which are different, or by interpreting charts and graphs. In the latter test, a graph may be printed in the test booklet which you are asked to use as the basis for answering questions.

4) Observation

A popular test for law-enforcement positions is the observation test. A picture is shown to you for several minutes, then taken away. Questions about the picture test your ability to observe both details and larger elements.

5) Following directions

In many positions in the public service, the employee must be able to carry out written instructions dependably and accurately. You may be given a chart with several columns, each column listing a variety of information. The questions require you to carry out directions involving the information given in the chart.

6) Skills and aptitudes

Performance tests effectively measure some manual skills and aptitudes. When the skill is one in which you are trained, such as typing or shorthand, you can practice. These tests are often very much like those given in business school or high school courses. For many of the other skills and aptitudes, however, no short-time preparation can be made. Skills and abilities natural to you or that you have developed throughout your lifetime are being tested.

Many of the general questions just described provide all the data needed to answer the questions and ask you to use your reasoning ability to find the answers. Your best preparation for these tests, as well as for tests of facts and ideas, is to be at your physical and mental best. You, no doubt, have your own methods of getting into an exam-taking mood and keeping "in shape." The next section lists some ideas on this subject.

IV. KINDS OF QUESTIONS

Only rarely is the "essay" question, which you answer in narrative form, used in civil service tests. Civil service tests are usually of the short-answer type. Full instructions for answering these questions will be given to you at the examination. But in case this is your first experience with short-answer questions and separate answer sheets, here is what you need to know:

1) Multiple-choice Questions

Most popular of the short-answer questions is the "multiple choice" or "best answer" question. It can be used, for example, to test for factual knowledge, ability to solve problems or judgment in meeting situations found at work.

A multiple-choice question is normally one of three types—
- It can begin with an incomplete statement followed by several possible endings. You are to find the one ending which *best* completes the statement, although some of the others may not be entirely wrong.
- It can also be a complete statement in the form of a question which is answered by choosing one of the statements listed.

- It can be in the form of a problem – again you select the best answer.

Here is an example of a multiple-choice question with a discussion which should give you some clues as to the method for choosing the right answer:

When an employee has a complaint about his assignment, the action which will *best* help him overcome his difficulty is to
   A. discuss his difficulty with his coworkers
   B. take the problem to the head of the organization
   C. take the problem to the person who gave him the assignment
   D. say nothing to anyone about his complaint

In answering this question, you should study each of the choices to find which is best. Consider choice "A" – Certainly an employee may discuss his complaint with fellow employees, but no change or improvement can result, and the complaint remains unresolved. Choice "B" is a poor choice since the head of the organization probably does not know what assignment you have been given, and taking your problem to him is known as "going over the head" of the supervisor. The supervisor, or person who made the assignment, is the person who can clarify it or correct any injustice. Choice "C" is, therefore, correct. To say nothing, as in choice "D," is unwise. Supervisors have and interest in knowing the problems employees are facing, and the employee is seeking a solution to his problem.

2) True/False Questions

The "true/false" or "right/wrong" form of question is sometimes used. Here a complete statement is given. Your job is to decide whether the statement is right or wrong.

SAMPLE: A roaming cell-phone call to a nearby city costs less than a non-roaming call to a distant city.

This statement is wrong, or false, since roaming calls are more expensive.

This is not a complete list of all possible question forms, although most of the others are variations of these common types. You will always get complete directions for answering questions. Be sure you understand *how* to mark your answers – ask questions until you do.

V. RECORDING YOUR ANSWERS

Computer terminals are used more and more today for many different kinds of exams.

For an examination with very few applicants, you may be told to record your answers in the test booklet itself. Separate answer sheets are much more common. If this separate answer sheet is to be scored by machine – and this is often the case – it is highly important that you mark your answers correctly in order to get credit.

An electronic scoring machine is often used in civil service offices because of the speed with which papers can be scored. Machine-scored answer sheets must be marked with a pencil, which will be given to you. This pencil has a high graphite content which responds to the electronic scoring machine. As a matter of fact, stray dots may register as answers, so do not let your pencil rest on the answer sheet while you are pondering the correct answer. Also, if your pencil lead breaks or is otherwise defective, ask for another.

Since the answer sheet will be dropped in a slot in the scoring machine, be careful not to bend the corners or get the paper crumpled.

The answer sheet normally has five vertical columns of numbers, with 30 numbers to a column. These numbers correspond to the question numbers in your test booklet. After each number, going across the page are four or five pairs of dotted lines. These short dotted lines have small letters or numbers above them. The first two pairs may also have a "T" or "F" above the letters. This indicates that the first two pairs only are to be used if the questions are of the true-false type. If the questions are multiple choice, disregard the "T" and "F" and pay attention only to the small letters or numbers.

Answer your questions in the manner of the sample that follows:

32. The largest city in the United States is
   A. Washington, D.C.
   B. New York City
   C. Chicago
   D. Detroit
   E. San Francisco

1) Choose the answer you think is best. (New York City is the largest, so "B" is correct.)
2) Find the row of dotted lines numbered the same as the question you are answering. (Find row number 32)
3) Find the pair of dotted lines corresponding to the answer. (Find the pair of lines under the mark "B.")
4) Make a solid black mark between the dotted lines.

VI. BEFORE THE TEST

Common sense will help you find procedures to follow to get ready for an examination. Too many of us, however, overlook these sensible measures. Indeed, nervousness and fatigue have been found to be the most serious reasons why applicants fail to do their best on civil service tests. Here is a list of reminders:

- Begin your preparation early – Don't wait until the last minute to go scurrying around for books and materials or to find out what the position is all about.
- Prepare continuously – An hour a night for a week is better than an all-night cram session. This has been definitely established. What is more, a night a week for a month will return better dividends than crowding your study into a shorter period of time.
- Locate the place of the exam – You have been sent a notice telling you when and where to report for the examination. If the location is in a different town or otherwise unfamiliar to you, it would be well to inquire the best route and learn something about the building.
- Relax the night before the test – Allow your mind to rest. Do not study at all that night. Plan some mild recreation or diversion; then go to bed early and get a good night's sleep.
- Get up early enough to make a leisurely trip to the place for the test – This way unforeseen events, traffic snarls, unfamiliar buildings, etc. will not upset you.
- Dress comfortably – A written test is not a fashion show. You will be known by number and not by name, so wear something comfortable.

- Leave excess paraphernalia at home – Shopping bags and odd bundles will get in your way. You need bring only the items mentioned in the official notice you received; usually everything you need is provided. Do not bring reference books to the exam. They will only confuse those last minutes and be taken away from you when in the test room.
- Arrive somewhat ahead of time – If because of transportation schedules you must get there very early, bring a newspaper or magazine to take your mind off yourself while waiting.
- Locate the examination room – When you have found the proper room, you will be directed to the seat or part of the room where you will sit. Sometimes you are given a sheet of instructions to read while you are waiting. Do not fill out any forms until you are told to do so; just read them and be prepared.
- Relax and prepare to listen to the instructions
- If you have any physical problem that may keep you from doing your best, be sure to tell the test administrator. If you are sick or in poor health, you really cannot do your best on the exam. You can come back and take the test some other time.

VII. AT THE TEST

The day of the test is here and you have the test booklet in your hand. The temptation to get going is very strong. Caution! There is more to success than knowing the right answers. You must know how to identify your papers and understand variations in the type of short-answer question used in this particular examination. Follow these suggestions for maximum results from your efforts:

1) Cooperate with the monitor

The test administrator has a duty to create a situation in which you can be as much at ease as possible. He will give instructions, tell you when to begin, check to see that you are marking your answer sheet correctly, and so on. He is not there to guard you, although he will see that your competitors do not take unfair advantage. He wants to help you do your best.

2) Listen to all instructions

Don't jump the gun! Wait until you understand all directions. In most civil service tests you get more time than you need to answer the questions. So don't be in a hurry. Read each word of instructions until you clearly understand the meaning. Study the examples, listen to all announcements and follow directions. Ask questions if you do not understand what to do.

3) Identify your papers

Civil service exams are usually identified by number only. You will be assigned a number; you must not put your name on your test papers. Be sure to copy your number correctly. Since more than one exam may be given, copy your exact examination title.

4) Plan your time

Unless you are told that a test is a "speed" or "rate of work" test, speed itself is usually not important. Time enough to answer all the questions will be provided, but this does not mean that you have all day. An overall time limit has been set. Divide the total time (in minutes) by the number of questions to determine the approximate time you have for each question.

5) Do not linger over difficult questions

If you come across a difficult question, mark it with a paper clip (useful to have along) and come back to it when you have been through the booklet. One caution if you do this – be sure to skip a number on your answer sheet as well. Check often to be sure that you have not lost your place and that you are marking in the row numbered the same as the question you are answering.

6) Read the questions

Be sure you know what the question asks! Many capable people are unsuccessful because they failed to *read* the questions correctly.

7) Answer all questions

Unless you have been instructed that a penalty will be deducted for incorrect answers, it is better to guess than to omit a question.

8) Speed tests

It is often better NOT to guess on speed tests. It has been found that on timed tests people are tempted to spend the last few seconds before time is called in marking answers at random – without even reading them – in the hope of picking up a few extra points. To discourage this practice, the instructions may warn you that your score will be "corrected" for guessing. That is, a penalty will be applied. The incorrect answers will be deducted from the correct ones, or some other penalty formula will be used.

9) Review your answers

If you finish before time is called, go back to the questions you guessed or omitted to give them further thought. Review other answers if you have time.

10) Return your test materials

If you are ready to leave before others have finished or time is called, take ALL your materials to the monitor and leave quietly. Never take any test material with you. The monitor can discover whose papers are not complete, and taking a test booklet may be grounds for disqualification.

VIII. EXAMINATION TECHNIQUES

1) Read the general instructions carefully. These are usually printed on the first page of the exam booklet. As a rule, these instructions refer to the timing of the examination; the fact that you should not start work until the signal and must stop work at a signal, etc. If there are any *special* instructions, such as a choice of questions to be answered, make sure that you note this instruction carefully.

2) When you are ready to start work on the examination, that is as soon as the signal has been given, read the instructions to each question booklet, underline any key words or phrases, such as *least, best, outline, describe* and the like. In this way you will tend to answer as requested rather than discover on reviewing your paper that you *listed without describing*, that you selected the *worst* choice rather than the *best* choice, etc.

3) If the examination is of the objective or multiple-choice type – that is, each question will also give a series of possible answers: A, B, C or D, and you are called upon to select the best answer and write the letter next to that answer on your answer paper – it is advisable to start answering each question in turn. There may be anywhere from 50 to 100 such questions in the three or four hours allotted and you can see how much time would be taken if you read through all the questions before beginning to answer any. Furthermore, if you come across a question or group of questions which you know would be difficult to answer, it would undoubtedly affect your handling of all the other questions.

4) If the examination is of the essay type and contains but a few questions, it is a moot point as to whether you should read all the questions before starting to answer any one. Of course, if you are given a choice – say five out of seven and the like – then it is essential to read all the questions so you can eliminate the two that are most difficult. If, however, you are asked to answer all the questions, there may be danger in trying to answer the easiest one first because you may find that you will spend too much time on it. The best technique is to answer the first question, then proceed to the second, etc.

5) Time your answers. Before the exam begins, write down the time it started, then add the time allowed for the examination and write down the time it must be completed, then divide the time available somewhat as follows:
    - If 3-1/2 hours are allowed, that would be 210 minutes. If you have 80 objective-type questions, that would be an average of 2-1/2 minutes per question. Allow yourself no more than 2 minutes per question, or a total of 160 minutes, which will permit about 50 minutes to review.
    - If for the time allotment of 210 minutes there are 7 essay questions to answer, that would average about 30 minutes a question. Give yourself only 25 minutes per question so that you have about 35 minutes to review.

6) The most important instruction is to *read each question* and make sure you know what is wanted. The second most important instruction is to *time yourself properly* so that you answer every question. The third most important instruction is to *answer every question*. Guess if you have to but include something for each question. Remember that you will receive no credit for a blank and will probably receive some credit if you write something in answer to an essay question. If you guess a letter – say "B" for a multiple-choice question – you may have guessed right. If you leave a blank as an answer to a multiple-choice question, the examiners may respect your feelings but it will not add a point to your score. Some exams may penalize you for wrong answers, so in such cases *only*, you may not want to guess unless you have some basis for your answer.

7) Suggestions
    a. Objective-type questions
        1. Examine the question booklet for proper sequence of pages and questions
        2. Read all instructions carefully
        3. Skip any question which seems too difficult; return to it after all other questions have been answered
        4. Apportion your time properly; do not spend too much time on any single question or group of questions

5. Note and underline key words – *all, most, fewest, least, best, worst, same, opposite*, etc.
6. Pay particular attention to negatives
7. Note unusual option, e.g., unduly long, short, complex, different or similar in content to the body of the question
8. Observe the use of "hedging" words – *probably, may, most likely*, etc.
9. Make sure that your answer is put next to the same number as the question
10. Do not second-guess unless you have good reason to believe the second answer is definitely more correct
11. Cross out original answer if you decide another answer is more accurate; do not erase until you are ready to hand your paper in
12. Answer all questions; guess unless instructed otherwise
13. Leave time for review

   b. Essay questions
1. Read each question carefully
2. Determine exactly what is wanted. Underline key words or phrases.
3. Decide on outline or paragraph answer
4. Include many different points and elements unless asked to develop any one or two points or elements
5. Show impartiality by giving pros and cons unless directed to select one side only
6. Make and write down any assumptions you find necessary to answer the questions
7. Watch your English, grammar, punctuation and choice of words
8. Time your answers; don't crowd material

8) Answering the essay question

Most essay questions can be answered by framing the specific response around several key words or ideas. Here are a few such key words or ideas:

M's: manpower, materials, methods, money, management
P's: purpose, program, policy, plan, procedure, practice, problems, pitfalls, personnel, public relations

   a. Six basic steps in handling problems:
1. Preliminary plan and background development
2. Collect information, data and facts
3. Analyze and interpret information, data and facts
4. Analyze and develop solutions as well as make recommendations
5. Prepare report and sell recommendations
6. Install recommendations and follow up effectiveness

   b. Pitfalls to avoid
1. *Taking things for granted* – A statement of the situation does not necessarily imply that each of the elements is necessarily true; for example, a complaint may be invalid and biased so that all that can be taken for granted is that a complaint has been registered

2. *Considering only one side of a situation* – Wherever possible, indicate several alternatives and then point out the reasons you selected the best one
3. *Failing to indicate follow up* – Whenever your answer indicates action on your part, make certain that you will take proper follow-up action to see how successful your recommendations, procedures or actions turn out to be
4. *Taking too long in answering any single question* – Remember to time your answers properly

IX. AFTER THE TEST

Scoring procedures differ in detail among civil service jurisdictions although the general principles are the same. Whether the papers are hand-scored or graded by machine we have described, they are nearly always graded by number. That is, the person who marks the paper knows only the number – never the name – of the applicant. Not until all the papers have been graded will they be matched with names. If other tests, such as training and experience or oral interview ratings have been given, scores will be combined. Different parts of the examination usually have different weights. For example, the written test might count 60 percent of the final grade, and a rating of training and experience 40 percent. In many jurisdictions, veterans will have a certain number of points added to their grades.

After the final grade has been determined, the names are placed in grade order and an eligible list is established. There are various methods for resolving ties between those who get the same final grade – probably the most common is to place first the name of the person whose application was received first. Job offers are made from the eligible list in the order the names appear on it. You will be notified of your grade and your rank as soon as all these computations have been made. This will be done as rapidly as possible.

People who are found to meet the requirements in the announcement are called "eligibles." Their names are put on a list of eligible candidates. An eligible's chances of getting a job depend on how high he stands on this list and how fast agencies are filling jobs from the list.

When a job is to be filled from a list of eligibles, the agency asks for the names of people on the list of eligibles for that job. When the civil service commission receives this request, it sends to the agency the names of the three people highest on this list. Or, if the job to be filled has specialized requirements, the office sends the agency the names of the top three persons who meet these requirements from the general list.

The appointing officer makes a choice from among the three people whose names were sent to him. If the selected person accepts the appointment, the names of the others are put back on the list to be considered for future openings.

That is the rule in hiring from all kinds of eligible lists, whether they are for typist, carpenter, chemist, or something else. For every vacancy, the appointing officer has his choice of any one of the top three eligibles on the list. This explains why the person whose name is on top of the list sometimes does not get an appointment when some of the persons lower on the list do. If the appointing officer chooses the second or third eligible, the No. 1 eligible does not get a job at once, but stays on the list until he is appointed or the list is terminated.

X. HOW TO PASS THE INTERVIEW TEST

The examination for which you applied requires an oral interview test. You have already taken the written test and you are now being called for the interview test – the final part of the formal examination.

You may think that it is not possible to prepare for an interview test and that there are no procedures to follow during an interview. Our purpose is to point out some things you can do in advance that will help you and some good rules to follow and pitfalls to avoid while you are being interviewed.

What is an interview supposed to test?

The written examination is designed to test the technical knowledge and competence of the candidate; the oral is designed to evaluate intangible qualities, not readily measured otherwise, and to establish a list showing the relative fitness of each candidate – as measured against his competitors – for the position sought. Scoring is not on the basis of "right" and "wrong," but on a sliding scale of values ranging from "not passable" to "outstanding." As a matter of fact, it is possible to achieve a relatively low score without a single "incorrect" answer because of evident weakness in the qualities being measured.

Occasionally, an examination may consist entirely of an oral test – either an individual or a group oral. In such cases, information is sought concerning the technical knowledges and abilities of the candidate, since there has been no written examination for this purpose. More commonly, however, an oral test is used to supplement a written examination.

Who conducts interviews?

The composition of oral boards varies among different jurisdictions. In nearly all, a representative of the personnel department serves as chairman. One of the members of the board may be a representative of the department in which the candidate would work. In some cases, "outside experts" are used, and, frequently, a businessman or some other representative of the general public is asked to serve. Labor and management or other special groups may be represented. The aim is to secure the services of experts in the appropriate field.

However the board is composed, it is a good idea (and not at all improper or unethical) to ascertain in advance of the interview who the members are and what groups they represent. When you are introduced to them, you will have some idea of their backgrounds and interests, and at least you will not stutter and stammer over their names.

What should be done before the interview?

While knowledge about the board members is useful and takes some of the surprise element out of the interview, there is other preparation which is more substantive. It *is* possible to prepare for an oral interview – in several ways:

1) Keep a copy of your application and review it carefully before the interview

This may be the only document before the oral board, and the starting point of the interview. Know what education and experience you have listed there, and the sequence and dates of all of it. Sometimes the board will ask you to review the highlights of your experience for them; you should not have to hem and haw doing it.

2) Study the class specification and the examination announcement

Usually, the oral board has one or both of these to guide them. The qualities, characteristics or knowledges required by the position sought are stated in these documents. They offer valuable clues as to the nature of the oral interview. For example, if the job involves supervisory responsibilities, the announcement will usually indicate that knowledge of modern supervisory methods and the qualifications of the candidate as a supervisor will be tested. If so, you can expect such questions, frequently in the form of a hypothetical situation which you are expected to solve. NEVER go into an oral without knowledge of the duties and responsibilities of the job you seek.

3) Think through each qualification required

Try to visualize the kind of questions you would ask if you were a board member. How well could you answer them? Try especially to appraise your own knowledge and background in each area, *measured against the job sought*, and identify any areas in which you are weak. Be critical and realistic – do not flatter yourself.

4) Do some general reading in areas in which you feel you may be weak

For example, if the job involves supervision and your past experience has NOT, some general reading in supervisory methods and practices, particularly in the field of human relations, might be useful. Do NOT study agency procedures or detailed manuals. The oral board will be testing your understanding and capacity, not your memory.

5) Get a good night's sleep and watch your general health and mental attitude

You will want a clear head at the interview. Take care of a cold or any other minor ailment, and of course, no hangovers.

What should be done on the day of the interview?

Now comes the day of the interview itself. Give yourself plenty of time to get there. Plan to arrive somewhat ahead of the scheduled time, particularly if your appointment is in the fore part of the day. If a previous candidate fails to appear, the board might be ready for you a bit early. By early afternoon an oral board is almost invariably behind schedule if there are many candidates, and you may have to wait. Take along a book or magazine to read, or your application to review, but leave any extraneous material in the waiting room when you go in for your interview. In any event, relax and compose yourself.

The matter of dress is important. The board is forming impressions about you – from your experience, your manners, your attitude, and your appearance. Give your personal appearance careful attention. Dress your best, but not your flashiest. Choose conservative, appropriate clothing, and be sure it is immaculate. This is a business interview, and your appearance should indicate that you regard it as such. Besides, being well groomed and properly dressed will help boost your confidence.

Sooner or later, someone will call your name and escort you into the interview room. *This is it*. From here on you are on your own. It is too late for any more preparation. But remember, you asked for this opportunity to prove your fitness, and you are here because your request was granted.

What happens when you go in?

The usual sequence of events will be as follows: The clerk (who is often the board stenographer) will introduce you to the chairman of the oral board, who will introduce you to the other members of the board. Acknowledge the introductions before you sit down. Do not be surprised if you find a microphone facing you or a stenotypist sitting by. Oral interviews are usually recorded in the event of an appeal or other review.

Usually the chairman of the board will open the interview by reviewing the highlights of your education and work experience from your application – primarily for the benefit of the other members of the board, as well as to get the material into the record. Do not interrupt or comment unless there is an error or significant misinterpretation; if that is the case, do not hesitate. But do not quibble about insignificant matters. Also, he will usually ask you some question about your education, experience or your present job – partly to get you to start talking and to establish the interviewing "rapport." He may start the actual questioning, or turn it over to one of the other members. Frequently, each member undertakes the questioning on a particular area, one in which he is perhaps most competent, so you can expect each member to participate in the examination. Because time is limited, you may also expect some rather abrupt switches in the direction the questioning takes, so do not be upset by it. Normally, a board member will not pursue a single line of questioning unless he discovers a particular strength or weakness.

After each member has participated, the chairman will usually ask whether any member has any further questions, then will ask you if you have anything you wish to add. Unless you are expecting this question, it may floor you. Worse, it may start you off on an extended, extemporaneous speech. The board is not usually seeking more information. The question is principally to offer you a last opportunity to present further qualifications or to indicate that you have nothing to add. So, if you feel that a significant qualification or characteristic has been overlooked, it is proper to point it out in a sentence or so. Do not compliment the board on the thoroughness of their examination – they have been sketchy, and you know it. If you wish, merely say, "No thank you, I have nothing further to add." This is a point where you can "talk yourself out" of a good impression or fail to present an important bit of information. Remember, *you close the interview yourself.*

The chairman will then say, "That is all, Mr. _____, thank you." Do not be startled; the interview is over, and quicker than you think. Thank him, gather your belongings and take your leave. Save your sigh of relief for the other side of the door.

How to put your best foot forward

Throughout this entire process, you may feel that the board individually and collectively is trying to pierce your defenses, seek out your hidden weaknesses and embarrass and confuse you. Actually, this is not true. They are obliged to make an appraisal of your qualifications for the job you are seeking, and they want to see you in your best light. Remember, they must interview all candidates and a non-cooperative candidate may become a failure in spite of their best efforts to bring out his qualifications. Here are 15 suggestions that will help you:

1) Be natural – Keep your attitude confident, not cocky

If you are not confident that you can do the job, do not expect the board to be. Do not apologize for your weaknesses, try to bring out your strong points. The board is interested in a positive, not negative, presentation. Cockiness will antagonize any board member and make him wonder if you are covering up a weakness by a false show of strength.

2) Get comfortable, but don't lounge or sprawl

Sit erectly but not stiffly. A careless posture may lead the board to conclude that you are careless in other things, or at least that you are not impressed by the importance of the occasion. Either conclusion is natural, even if incorrect. Do not fuss with your clothing, a pencil or an ashtray. Your hands may occasionally be useful to emphasize a point; do not let them become a point of distraction.

3) Do not wisecrack or make small talk

This is a serious situation, and your attitude should show that you consider it as such. Further, the time of the board is limited – they do not want to waste it, and neither should you.

4) Do not exaggerate your experience or abilities
In the first place, from information in the application or other interviews and sources, the board may know more about you than you think. Secondly, you probably will not get away with it. An experienced board is rather adept at spotting such a situation, so do not take the chance.

5) If you know a board member, do not make a point of it, yet do not hide it
Certainly you are not fooling him, and probably not the other members of the board. Do not try to take advantage of your acquaintanceship – it will probably do you little good.

6) Do not dominate the interview
Let the board do that. They will give you the clues – do not assume that you have to do all the talking. Realize that the board has a number of questions to ask you, and do not try to take up all the interview time by showing off your extensive knowledge of the answer to the first one.

7) Be attentive
You only have 20 minutes or so, and you should keep your attention at its sharpest throughout. When a member is addressing a problem or question to you, give him your undivided attention. Address your reply principally to him, but do not exclude the other board members.

8) Do not interrupt
A board member may be stating a problem for you to analyze. He will ask you a question when the time comes. Let him state the problem, and wait for the question.

9) Make sure you understand the question
Do not try to answer until you are sure what the question is. If it is not clear, restate it in your own words or ask the board member to clarify it for you. However, do not haggle about minor elements.

10) Reply promptly but not hastily
A common entry on oral board rating sheets is "candidate responded readily," or "candidate hesitated in replies." Respond as promptly and quickly as you can, but do not jump to a hasty, ill-considered answer.

11) Do not be peremptory in your answers
A brief answer is proper – but do not fire your answer back. That is a losing game from your point of view. The board member can probably ask questions much faster than you can answer them.

12) Do not try to create the answer you think the board member wants
He is interested in what kind of mind you have and how it works – not in playing games. Furthermore, he can usually spot this practice and will actually grade you down on it.

13) Do not switch sides in your reply merely to agree with a board member
Frequently, a member will take a contrary position merely to draw you out and to see if you are willing and able to defend your point of view. Do not start a debate, yet do not surrender a good position. If a position is worth taking, it is worth defending.

14) Do not be afraid to admit an error in judgment if you are shown to be wrong

The board knows that you are forced to reply without any opportunity for careful consideration. Your answer may be demonstrably wrong. If so, admit it and get on with the interview.

15) Do not dwell at length on your present job

The opening question may relate to your present assignment. Answer the question but do not go into an extended discussion. You are being examined for a *new* job, not your present one. As a matter of fact, try to phrase ALL your answers in terms of the job for which you are being examined.

Basis of Rating

Probably you will forget most of these "do's" and "don'ts" when you walk into the oral interview room. Even remembering them all will not ensure you a passing grade. Perhaps you did not have the qualifications in the first place. But remembering them will help you to put your best foot forward, without treading on the toes of the board members.

Rumor and popular opinion to the contrary notwithstanding, an oral board wants you to make the best appearance possible. They know you are under pressure – but they also want to see how you respond to it as a guide to what your reaction would be under the pressures of the job you seek. They will be influenced by the degree of poise you display, the personal traits you show and the manner in which you respond.

ABOUT THIS BOOK

This book contains tests divided into Examination Sections. Go through each test, answering every question in the margin. We have also attached a sample answer sheet at the back of the book that can be removed and used. At the end of each test look at the answer key and check your answers. On the ones you got wrong, look at the right answer choice and learn. Do not fill in the answers first. Do not memorize the questions and answers, but understand the answer and principles involved. On your test, the questions will likely be different from the samples. Questions are changed and new ones added. If you understand these past questions you should have success with any changes that arise. Tests may consist of several types of questions. We have additional books on each subject should more study be advisable or necessary for you. Finally, the more you study, the better prepared you will be. This book is intended to be the last thing you study before you walk into the examination room. Prior study of relevant texts is also recommended. NLC publishes some of these in our Fundamental Series. Knowledge and good sense are important factors in passing your exam. Good luck also helps. So now study this Passbook, absorb the material contained within and take that knowledge into the examination. Then do your best to pass that exam.

EXAMINATION SECTION

EXAMINATION SECTION
TEST 1

DIRECTIONS: Each question or incomplete statement is followed by several suggested answers or completions. Select the one that BEST answers the question or completes the statement. *PRINT THE LETTER OF THE CORRECT ANSWER IN THE SPACE AT THE RIGHT.*

1. A steam heating boiler is classified as a low pressure boiler when it generates steam at a gage pressure of

    A. not more than 30 pounds per square inch
    B. not more than 25 pounds per square inch
    C. not more than 20 pounds per square inch
    D. 15 pounds per square inch or less

1.____

2. A hot water heating boiler is classified as a low pressure boiler when it produces hot water at a gage pressure

    A. not more than 200 pounds per square inch
    B. not more than 175 pounds per square inch
    C. not more than 160 pounds per square inch
    D. equal to an absolute pressure of 200 pounds per square inch

2.____

3. Of the following processes, the one which is NOT involved in the transfer of heat in a boiler from the hot gases to the water is

    A. radiation   B. conduction
    C. convection   D. evaporation

3.____

4. The MINIMUM flue gas CO_2 reading permitted in a large metropolitan city is

    A. 5%   B. 8%   C. 12%   D. 16%

4.____

5. The Ringelmann Chart is a device that is used for checking

    A. smoke density from a chimney
    B. boiler water condition
    C. percent CO_2 of the flue gas
    D. the carbon content of coal

5.____

6. Low voltage control circuits for oil burners usually operate at a voltage of _____ volts.

    A. six (6)   B. twelve (12)
    C. twenty-five (25)   D. fifty (50)

6.____

7. The connection known as a *Hartford Loop* is usually found on

    A. radiators
    B. high pressure hot water heaters
    C. low pressure unit heaters
    D. low pressure steam boilers

7.____

8. Of the following types of fuel oils, the one that has the GREATEST heat value per gallon is _____ oil.

   A. diesel   B. #2   C. #4   D. #6

9. Of the following types of fuel, the one which has the HIGHEST heat content per pound (Btu/lb) is

   A. #2 fuel oil
   B. semibituminous coal
   C. semianthracite coal
   D. wood

10. The atomization of oil in the average domestic gun-type burner is accomplished by the

    A. air pressure
    B. pressure and centrifugal action of the oil
    C. low steam pressure
    D. draft effect of the stack

11. The type of fuel oil pump MOST commonly used with gun-type oil burners is the _____ type.

    A. centrifugal
    B. external or internal gear
    C. volute
    D. propeller

12. Chimney draft is usually measured in

    A. inches of mercury
    B. inches of water
    C. feet of water
    D. pounds per square inch

13. *Draft* that is produced over the fire or in a chimney without the use of any mechanical aids is generally known as _____ draft.

    A. balanced
    B. induced
    C. positive
    D. natural

14. Assume that a residential heating control system consists of a room thermostat, a limit control, a combustion control, a safety control, and a control relay. These controls would MOST likely be used with

    A. automatic gas-fired burners
    B. automatic oil-fired burners
    C. coal-fired stokers
    D. electric heating systems

15. A gauge that can be used for measuring either a vacuum or positive pressure in pounds per square inch is generally called a _____ gauge.

    A. compound
    B. pressure
    C. boiler
    D. vacuum

16. The purpose of a goose-neck connection to a Bourdon type steam gage is to

    A. prevent water getting into the gage tube
    B. prevent steam getting into the gage tube
    C. correct for trapped air in the line
    D. allow impurities to settle in the tube

17. The device that is generally used to reduce high pressure steam to low pressure steam is called a

    A. pressure relief valve
    B. pressure regulating valve
    C. condenser
    D. by-pass control valve

18. The MAXIMUM size of boiler safety valve that can be used on a low pressure boiler is

    A. 2"   B. $3\frac{1}{2}$"   C. $4\frac{1}{2}$"   D. $5\frac{1}{2}$"

19. If the water level in a steam heating boiler is unsteady, the probable cause may MOST likely be due to

    A. overfiring of boiler
    B. the use of a poor grade of fuel
    C. insufficient radiation in the heating system
    D. the use of an oversized boiler

20. The PRIMARY reason for using a gate valve in low pressure steam lines is to

    A. vary the steam pressure
    B. allow for quick opening
    C. reduce the flow of condensate to the boiler
    D. allow full free flow

21. Of the following types of valves, the one which is generally used to allow fluids to flow in one direction only is the

    A. gas cock   B. globe valve
    C. check valve   D. by-pass valve

22. The type of valve that is usually in a line with a swing check valve is a _____ valve.

    A. gate   B. diaphragm
    C. quick opening   D. globe

23. Excessive use of highly alkaline water in a boiler would probably result in boiler

    A. caustic embrittlement   B. priming
    C. foaming   D. corrosion

24. In a fire tube boiler, most of the soot usually accumulates

    A. on the inside surface of the tubes
    B. on the bridge wall
    C. in the combustion chamber
    D. on the outside surface of the tubes

25. Pneumatic tools are usually operated by

    A. steam   B. air   C. water   D. electricity

26. An *intercooler* is a device usually used in conjunction with a(n)

    A. boiler
    B. gear type oil pump
    C. centrifugal water pump
    D. air compressor

27. Of the following types of boilers, the one that is MOST commonly used for low pressure steam operation is the _____ boiler.

    A. Stirling
    B. cross-drum straight-tube
    C. cast iron vertical header logitudinal
    D. fire tube

28. The sum of the following pipe lengths, 15 5/8", 8 3/4", 30 5/6", and 20 1/2", is *most nearly*

    A. 77 1/8"   B. 76 3/16"   C. 75 3/16"   D. 74 5/16"

29. A boiler shell can sometimes be repaired temporarily by means of a

    A. soft patch and patch bolt
    B. hard patch and cap screws
    C. hard patch and rivets
    D. soft patch and rivets

30. The method generally used to provide rigidity for the internal flat surfaces of horizontal fire tube boilers is by

    A. riveting   B. staying   C. welding   D. caulking

31. The function of try-cocks on a boiler is PRIMARILY to

    A. drain the gage glass
    B. add water to the boiler
    C. check the gage glass reading
    D. blow down the water column

32. A boiler *blow-off* is usually connected

    A. to the steam compartment of the boiler
    B. next to the water column
    C. to the lowest water space available
    D. to the Hartford Loop

33. A boiler feedwater regulator automatically controls the

    A. water temperature in the boiler
    B. water pressure to the boiler
    C. feedwater treatment to the boiler
    D. water supply to the boiler

34. A feedwater heater in a steam generating plant is generally used to

    A. heat and condition water to the boiler
    B. provide make-up steam for the boiler
    C. feed hot water to plumbing fixtures
    D. increase feedwater pressure

35. If the outside diameter of a pipe is 6 inches and the wall thickness is $\frac{1}{2}$ inch, the inside area of this pipe, in square inches, is *most nearly*

   A. 15.7 B. 17.3 C. 19.6 D. 23.8

36. The type of pipe, used for water or gas, that should NOT be welded is _____ pipe.

   A. galvanized
   B. brass
   C. black wrought iron
   D. black steel

37. The instrument usually used to calibrate steam pressure gages is known as a _____ tester.

   A. lever-arm weight
   B. dead-weight
   C. Fyrite
   D. calibrated spring scale

38. A boiler horsepower is the evaporation from and at 212°F of _____ pounds of water per hour.

   A. 34.50 B. 30.50 C. 29.50 D. 25.50

39. A steam heating system that operates under both vacuum and low pressure conditions without use of a vacuum pump is known as a _____ system.

   A. forced return
   B. low pressure
   C. vacuum
   D. vapor

40. The purpose of an expansion tank in a hot water heating system is to

   A. add cold water to the system when needed
   B. prevent water hammer in the system
   C. allow for changes in the volume of water in the system
   D. store the water of the system when boiler is off the line

KEY (CORRECT ANSWERS)

1. D	11. B	21. C	31. C
2. C	12. B	22. A	32. C
3. D	13. D	23. A	33. D
4. B	14. B	24. A	34. A
5. A	15. A	25. B	35. C
6. C	16. B	26. D	36. A
7. D	17. B	27. D	37. B
8. D	18. C	28. C	38. A
9. A	19. A	29. A	39. D
10. B	20. D	30. B	40. C

TEST 2

DIRECTIONS: Each question or incomplete statement is followed by several suggested answers or completions. Select the one that BEST answers the question or completes the statement. *PRINT THE LETTER OF THE CORRECT ANSWER IN THE SPACE AT THE RIGHT.*

1. The pressure relief valve in a forced hot water heating system is generally mounted   1._____

    A. on top of the boiler
    B. on top of the air cushion tank
    C. in the hot water return line
    D. on the line between the circulating pump and the boiler

2. In a forced hot water circulating system, the circulating pump is usually controlled by a   2._____

    A. low-water cut out   B. room thermostat
    C. return-pump control   D. float

3. The diameter of a roof vent from an open expansion tank in a hot water heating system should be NOT less than   3._____

    A. 5"   B. 4"   C. 3"   D. 2"

4. If the circumference of a circle measures 12.566 inches, its diameter is equal to *most nearly*   4._____

    A. 2.75"   B. 3.00"   C. 3.50"   D. 4.00"

5. A valve that opens when its solenoid is energized and closes when the current is interrupted is known as a _____ valve.   5._____

    A. magnetic   B. thermostatic
    C. relay   D. shut-off

6. The device that shuts off the flow of fuel oil to a rotary cup type oil burner, in case of primary air failure, is generally known as a   6._____

    A. flame supervisor   B. pressuretrol
    C. aquastat   D. vaporstat

7. A device used to assure a proper temperature of No. 6 fuel oil before it is allowed to enter a burner is known as a   7._____

    A. thermostat   B. aquastat
    C. pyrostat   D. fustat

8. A device used to start the operation of line voltage equipment by means of a low voltage control circuit is called a   8._____

    A. circuit breaker   B. relay
    C. rectifier   D. variac

9. A pyrometer is generally used to measure the   9._____

    A. specific gravity of a liquid
    B. density of a gas

C. temperature of flue gas
D. percent of carbon dioxide

10. A low water cut-off on a boiler is usually operated by means of a   10.____

    A. bellows   B. helix   C. float   D. diaphragm

11. Assume that the water level in the gauge glass of a steaming boiler drops out of sight   11.____
    during a test of the low water cut-off.
    As an inspector, you

    A. order the boiler to be taken off the line
    B. assume the cut-off is working properly
    C. order more water to be put into the boiler
    D. order the drain valves to be opened immediately

12. The function of a *pressuretrol* on an oil-fired steam boiler is to keep the   12.____

    A. oil pressure constant
    B. steam pressure from exceeding a predetermined amount
    C. water pressure above 20 pounds per square inch
    D. draft pressure below atmosphere

13. A *remote control switch* for an oil burner should usually be located   13.____

    A. next to the three-way magnetic oil valve
    B. only at the boiler
    C. at the exit of the boiler room
    D. in the superintendent's office

14. A stack switch is a device that is used to shut off the oil burner in case of   14.____

    A. flame failure
    B. high steam pressure
    C. excessive flue gas temperature
    D. low water in boiler

15. A pressuretrol is usually connected directly to the   15.____

    A. water side of a boiler
    B. flue gas side of a boiler
    C. steam side of a boiler
    D. discharge side of fuel line

16. A modutrol motor on a typical automatic oil burner firing #6 oil may be used to directly 16.____
    control the

    A. speed of the oil pump or vaporstat
    B. primary air, secondary air, and oil control valve
    C. 3-way magnetic oil valve and magnetic gas valve
    D. electric fuel oil preheater and aquastat

Questions 17-20.

DIRECTIONS: Questions 17 to 20 inclusive are to be answered by referring to the drawing symbols of screwed fittings and valves shown below.

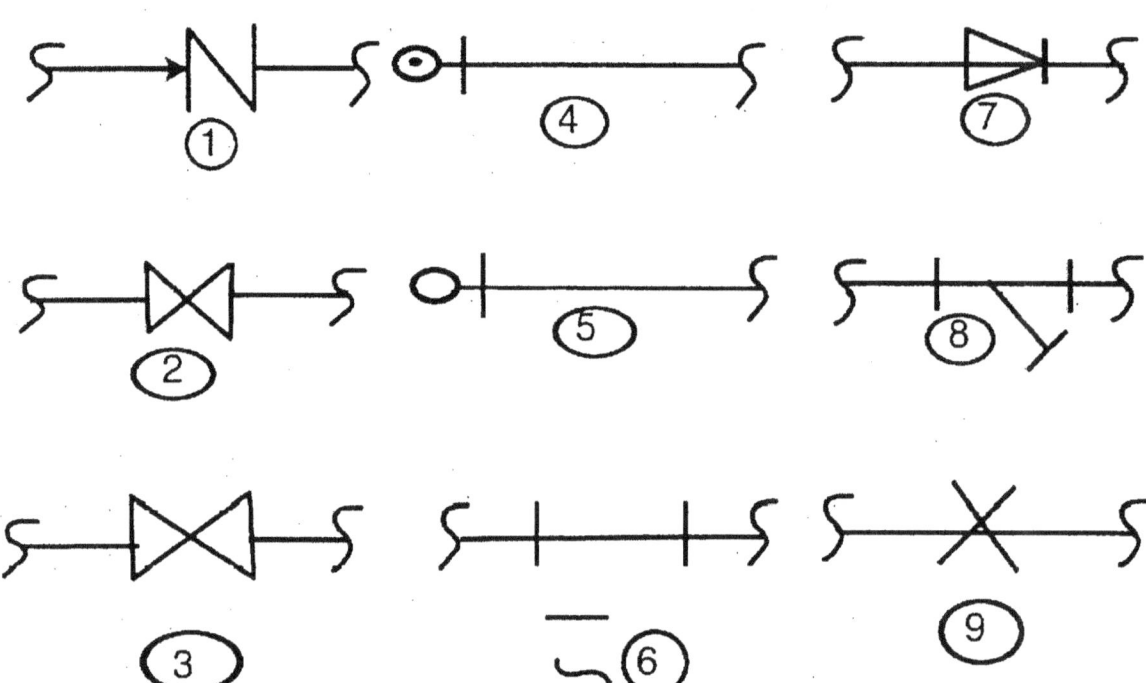

17. Referring to the above sketches, the one representing a turned-up elbow is numbered

    A. 4   B. 5   C. 6   D. 8

18. Referring to the above sketches, the one representing a check valve is numbered

    A. 1   B. 3   C. 7   D. 9

19. Referring to the above sketches, the one representing a globe valve is numbered

    A. 9   B. 3   C. 2   D. 1

20. Referring to the above sketches, the one representing a strainer is numbered

    A. 3   B. 7   C. 9   D. 8

21. The minimum size of pipe that should be used to connect a water column to a low pressure steam boiler is *most nearly*

    A. 3/8"   B. 1/2"   C. 3/4"   D. 1"

22. Of the following metals, the one which is classified as a ferrous metal is

    A. lead   B. iron   C. tin   D. zinc

23. Of the following types of pipe, the one which will expand the MOST when heated is

    A. copper   B. wrought iron
    C. steel   D. brass

24. Of the following devices, the ones that are usually used to provide for expansion in a long horizontal run of hot water pipe are

    A. clamps
    B. anchors
    C. swivel offsets
    D. pipe stanchions

25. The MINIMUM diameter of pipe that may be used for gas piping is

    A. 3/4"   B. 5/8"   C. 1/2"   D. 3/8"

26. The type of thread that is used on standard iron pipe size brass pipe is known as the

    A. Witworth Standard
    B. Briggs Standard
    C. British Association
    D. Standard Acme

27. The taper on a standard pipe thread is *most nearly* _____ to the foot.

    A. 1/8"   B. 1/4"   C. 1/2"   D. 3/4"

28. Of the following statements concerning the use of lamp wick on screwed pipe joints, the one which is *most nearly* CORRECT is that

    A. it may suggest the existence of imperfect threads
    B. it is the best modern day practice
    C. the joints are strengthened
    D. pipe compound is not needed

29. Of the following wrenches, the one which is used MOST often for making up connections to a boiler is the _____ wrench.

    A. monkey   B. open end   C. strap   D. pipe

30. Boiler fusible plugs are usually filled with

    A. lead   B. copper   C. tin   D. solder

31. The capacity, in gallons, of a 10'-0" diameter by 21'-0" high cylindrical tank with flat heads is *most nearly*

    A. 1650   B. 2100   C. 6900   D. 12,500

32. "The water level in the gage glass was *dormant* during the peak load conditions." As used in this sentence, the word *dormant* means *most nearly*

    A. fluctuating
    B. inactive
    C. clean
    D. foaming

33. The instructor's words were understood but *irrelevant*. As used in this sentence, the word *irrelevant* means *most nearly*

    A. unchallenging to the audience
    B. unconvincing to the audience
    C. not bearing upon the subject under discussion
    D. not based upon facts

34. The MOST important requirement of a good inspectional report is that it should be

    A. properly addressed
    B. lengthy
    C. clear and brief
    D. spelled correctly

35. Building superintendents frequently inquire about departmental inspectional procedures. Of the following, it is BEST to

   A. advise them to write to the department for an official reply
   B. refuse as the inspectional procedure is a restricted matter
   C. briefly explain the procedure to them
   D. avoid the inquiry by changing the subject

36. In making an inspection of a boiler repair job in progress in a private building, an inspector's PRIMARY concern should be to

   A. avoid conversation with the building superintendent
   B. concentrate on the workmanship of the men
   C. anticipate construction problems before they occur
   D. ascertain whether or not the repair job is in accordance with the code and regulations of the department

Questions 37-40.

DIRECTIONS: Questions 37 to 40, inclusive, are to be answered in accordance with the following paragraph.

A low pressure hot water boiler shall include a relief valve or valves of a capacity such that with the heat generating equipment operating at maximum, the pressure cannot rise more than 20 percent above the maximum allowable working pressure (set pressure) if that is 30 p.s.i. gage or less, nor more than 10 percent if it is more than 30 p.s.i. gage. The difference between the set pressure and the pressure at which the valve is relieving is known as "overpressure or accumulation." If the steam relieving capacity in pounds per hour is calculated, it shall be determined by dividing by 1,000 the maximum Btu output at the boiler nozzle obtainable from the heat generating equipment, or by multiplying the square feet of heating surface by five.

37. In accordance with the above paragraph, the capacity of a relief valve should be computed on the basis of

   A. size of boiler
   B. maximum rated capacity of generating equipment
   C. average output of the generating equipment
   D. minimum capacity of generating equipment

38. In accordance with the above paragraph, with a set pressure of 30 p.s.i. gage, the overpressure should NOT be more than _____ p.s.i.

   A. 3   B. 6   C. 33   D. 36

39. In accordance with the above paragraph, a relief valve should start relieving at a pressure equal to the _____ pressure.

   A. set
   B. over
   C. overpressure minus set
   D. set pressure plus over

40. In accordance with the above paragraph, the steam relieving capacity can be computed by 40.____
    A. multiplying the maximum BTU output by 5
    B. dividing the pounds of steam per hour by 1000
    C. dividing the maximum BTU output by the square feet of heating surface
    D. dividing the maximum BTU output by 1000

KEY (CORRECT ANSWERS)

1. A	11. A	21. D	31. D
2. B	12. B	22. B	32. B
3. B	13. C	23. A	33. C
4. D	14. A	24. C	34. C
5. A	15. C	25. D	35. C
6. D	16. B	26. B	36. D
7. B	17. A	27. D	37. B
8. B	18. A	28. A	38. B
9. C	19. B	29. D	39. D
10. C	20. D	30. C	40. D

EXAMINATION SECTION
TEST 1

DIRECTIONS: Each question or incomplete statement is followed by several suggested answers or completions. Select the one that BEST answers the question or completes the statement. *PRINT THE LETTER OF THE CORRECT ANSWER IN THE SPACE AT THE RIGHT.*

1. According to the Building Code, all boilers, including chimney connections, shall be inspected

    A. every six months
    B. yearly
    C. every two years
    D. every five years

    1.____

2. A boiler may not begin operating until a(n) _____ has been issued by the commissioner.

    A. certificate of compliance
    B. certificate of fitness
    C. equipment use permit
    D. all of the above

    2.____

3. All liquid fuel piping and fuel storage tanks must be _____ tested before the system is operated.

    A. electronically
    B. hydraulically
    C. hydrostatically
    D. all of the above

    3.____

4. Of the following, the person who is responsible for testing new equipment is the

    A. installing contractor
    B. public inspector
    C. fire prevention inspector
    D. owner of the building

    4.____

5. Piping must be tested at _____ times the maximum working pressure applicable to that part of the system.

    A. 1.5   B. 2   C. 5   D. 10

    5.____

6. The MINIMUM pressure for testing storage tanks is _____ the maximum working pressure of the tank, but not less than _____ psi.

    A. 1.5; 100   B. 5; 100   C. 1.5; 25   D. 5; 25

    6.____

7. The MINIMUM time for retaining testing conditions is

    A. 30 minutes
    B. one hour
    C. 6 hours
    D. 12 hours

    7.____

8. Records of pressure testing must be kept indicating the

    A. date and time of inspection
    B. date and name of the contractor
    C. name of the contractor and testing pressures
    D. date and testing pressures

    8.____

9. All oil burning systems must have a(n) _____ permanently located in an easily visible and accessible location.

   A. hydrostatic test kit
   B. instruction card
   C. fire extinguisher
   D. first-aid kit

10. Approval for the storage of fuel oil is given by the

    A. fire prevention inspector
    B. fire commissioner
    C. installing contractor
    D. none of the above

11. All oil burning systems must meet the requirements of the _____ code.

    A. fire safety
    B. air pollution control
    C. fuel efficiency
    D. all of the above

12. Unless a system is fully automatic, requiring no preheating, a(n) _____ must be in the building at all times while the burners are operating.

    A. person holding a certificate of fitness from the fire commissioner
    B. member of the local fire company
    C. automatic fire extinguishing system
    D. person with first aid certification

13. After any repairs to equipment requiring a licensed or qualified operator, such operator must check the

    A. repairs
    B. functioning of all control devices
    C. position of all valves
    D. all of the above

14. Equipment that is required to meet the standards of the air pollution control code includes

    A. all equipment burning solid, liquid, or gas fuels
    B. incinerators
    C. rubbish burners
    D. all of the above

15. Of the following, the one that is NOT an equipment classification is _____ temperature equipment.

    A. very high   B. high   C. medium   D. low

16. Ventilation must be capable of providing AT LEAST _____ required to fire the equipment to gross output.

    A. 50 cfm of air per gallon per hour
    B. 36 cfm of air per gallon per hour
    C. 50 psi per hour
    D. none of the above

17. All of the following are commercial grades of fuel oil EXCEPT No.

   A. 1   B. 4   C. 6   D. 8

18. Number 2 fuel oil is also known as _____ oil.

   A. range
   C. crankcase
   B. diesel
   D. none of the above

19. Acceptable fuel oils may NOT have a flashpoint of _____ F.

   A. above 100
   C. below 100
   B. above 180
   D. below 180

20. All of the following are acceptable as fuel in oil burning systems EXCEPT _____ oil.

   A. diesel
   C. range
   B. crankcase refuse
   D. none of the above

21. Oil in storage tanks may be heated by all of the following EXCEPT

   A. electric heaters
   C. gas heaters
   B. hot water
   D. steam

22. All oil burning systems must have a(n)

   A. remote control to stop the flow of oil to burners
   B. heating coil to preheat oil
   C. overflow pipe
   D. all of the above

23. Pressure in a storage tank for the purpose of discharging oil

   A. may not exceed 35 psi
   C. may not exceed 25 psi
   B. is prohibited
   D. is acceptable

24. Of the following, acceptable safety controls on an automatic burner may be of the _____ type.

   A. electric
   C. hydraulic
   B. pneumatic
   D. all of the above

25. Safety controls must provide all of the following functions EXCEPT

   A. emission control
   B. ignition
   C. stack or combustion control
   D. high temperature or pressure control

26. All oil burners must be connected to a(n)

   A. fire department relay
   C. catalytic converter
   B. chimney
   D. overflow pipe

27. The temperature in an oil storage tank is USUALLY maintained at _____ °F.

   A. 80   B. 90-120   C. 100-130   D. 120-140

28. Oil is circulated through the system by means of a(n)

    A. fuel injector
    B. suction pump
    C. pressure pump
    D. all of the above

29. _____ is(are) the MOST common contaminant(s) found in fuel oil.

    A. Ash
    B. Silicon carbide
    C. Dirt and sediment
    D. Shale

30. The *vacuum gauge* measures pressures

    A. above 100 psi
    B. between 25-100 psi
    C. above 50 psi
    D. below atmospheric

31. Unusually high vacuum readings may indicate

    A. inefficient operation
    B. an obstruction
    C. a dirty oil strainer
    D. all of the above

32. Prior to combustion, oils are GENERALLY heated to _____ °F.

    A. 120-150   B. 160-180   C. 180-200   D. 200-220

33. Atonized oil is mixed with _____ in the combustion chamber before it is burned.

    A. air   B. CO_2 C. water   D. liquid gas

34. In the event of ignition or combustion failure, the

    A. relief valves will open
    B. burner system will shut down
    C. relief valves will close
    D. none of the above

35. The normal oil pressure for #6 oil burners is _____ psi.

    A. 20-40   B. 70   C. 30-50   D. 25

36. Fuel oil is atomized prior to ignition and combustion in order to

    A. allow mixing with air
    B. ensure rapid combustion
    C. ensure prompt ignition
    D. all of the above

37. The combustible elements in fuel oil are

    A. carbon and oxygen
    B. carbon and hydrogen
    C. oxygen and nitrogen
    D. hydrogen and nitrogen

38. The end result of combustion is the

    A. burning of the fuel oil
    B. release of chemical elements
    C. production of heat energy
    D. all of the above

39. The carbon content of fuel oil is APPROXIMATELY

   A. 85%   B. 50%   C. 75%   D. 25%

40. The hydrogen content of fuel oil is APPROXIMATELY _____ %.

   A. 1   B. 14   C. 25   D. 85

KEY (CORRECT ANSWERS)

1.	B	11.	B	21.	C	31.	D
2.	C	12.	A	22.	A	32.	B
3.	C	13.	D	23.	B	33.	A
4.	A	14.	D	24.	D	34.	B
5.	A	15.	A	25.	A	35.	C
6.	C	16.	B	26.	B	36.	D
7.	A	17.	D	27.	C	37.	B
8.	C	18.	B	28.	B	38.	C
9.	B	19.	C	29.	C	39.	A
10.	B	20.	B	30.	D	40.	B

TEST 2

DIRECTIONS: Each question or incomplete statement is followed by several suggested answers or completions. Select the one that BEST answers the question or completes the statement. *PRINT THE LETTER OF THE CORRECT ANSWER IN THE SPACE AT THE RIGHT.*

1. The toxic gas that is formed during incomplete combustion is   1.____

    A. carbon monoxide B. carbon dioxide
    C. hydrogen dioxide D. carbolic acid

2. The efficiency of combustion is directly related to the   2.____

    A. amount of fuel oil atomized
    B. carbon/hydrogen ratio
    C. amount of oxygen mixed with the oil
    D. all of the above

3. Before oil will burn, it must be   3.____

    A. heated
    B. converted to a vapor or gas
    C. pressurized
    D. all of the above

4. The end product of complete combustion is   4.____

    A. carbon dioxide B. carbon monoxide
    C. hydrogen dioxide D. hydrogen sulfide

5. In low pressure oil burners, the combustion mixture is delivered to the combustion chamber at pressures between _____ psi.   5.____

    A. 10-20 B. 1-15 C. 20-40 D. 15-30

6. The air that makes contact with oil prior to leaving the nozzle is termed _____ air.   6.____

    A. combustion B. initial
    C. essential D. primary

7. Air that is introduced into the combustion chamber is terned _____ air.   7.____

    A. combustion B. secondary
    C. direct D. none of the above

8. Oil burners require APPROXIMATELY _____ cubic feet of air per gallon of oil burned.   8.____

    A. 1000 B. 1500 C. 2000 D. 2500

9. The *combustion chamber* is also referred to as the   9.____

    A. burn center B. firebox
    C. burnbox D. all of the above

10. The term BTU is used to measure   10.____

    A. combustion efficiency B. toxic emissions
    C. heat output D. none of the above

18

11. When one pound of carbon is burned under ideal conditions, _____ BTUs are released.

    A. 5000   B. 12,144   C. 15,455   D. 14,544

12. When carbon monoxide is formed as a product of combustion, _____ BTUs are liberated.

    A. 2450   B. 4480   C. 14,544   D. 15,455

13. A correctly adjusted oil burner flame will be

    A. orange with red tips
    B. red and smoky
    C. white
    D. blue

14. All of the following will result from an insufficient air supply EXCEPT

    A. black smoke
    B. soot
    C. flame blows out
    D. none of the above

15. Oil spray contacting the combustion chamber walls will

    A. burn most efficiently
    B. evaporate completely
    C. cause a smoky fire
    D. result in an explosive condition

16. The walls of the combustion chamber are made of

    A. stainless steel
    B. insulating firebrick
    C. tempered iron
    D. magnesium

17. The mixture in the combustion chamber is burned MOST efficiently by

    A. reflected heat
    B. contact with a heated surface
    C. contact with a flame
    D. none of the above

18. Once combustion has begun, the ignition

    A. maintains the fire
    B. is turned off
    C. begins a modified cycle
    D. none of the above

19. *Bunker C oil* or residual fuel oil is another name for # _____ fuel oil.

    A. 2   B. 4   C. 1   D. 6

20. Number _____ oil contains the MOST sediment.

    A. 6   B. 4   C. 2   D. 1

21. A defective oil cutoff valve can lead to

    A. afterdrip
    B. noisy burner start-up
    C. carbon deposit build-up
    D. all of the above

22. Nozzles in a #6 oil burner should be cleaned

    A. daily
    B. weekly
    C. monthly
    D. every six months

23. Blockage in the chimney or flue will cause

    A. inefficient combustion
    B. a fire hazard
    C. a smoke-filled boiler room
    D. all of the above

24. Vaporized oil will appear

    A. yellowish
    B. gray
    C. pure white
    D. pink

25. Delay in ignition of the fuel mixture is the MOST common cause of

    A. puffback
    B. fires
    C. inefficient combustion
    D. all of the above

26. Water in the fuel oil will result in

    A. highly efficient combustion
    B. an explosion hazard
    C. a fire hazard
    D. none of the above

27. The device that will shut down the oil burner if no air is available for combustion is the

    A. vacuum gauge
    B. vaporstat
    C. fuel valve
    D. stack switch

28. After ignition, combustion is maintained by

    A. a pilot flame
    B. a heating coil
    C. retained heat
    D. all of the above

29. The *photoelectric cell* is a(n) _____ control.

    A. vapor sensing
    B. flame detection
    C. atomizing
    D. pressure sensitive

30. If atomized oil is pumped into the combustion chamber, but not burned, _____ may result.

    A. carbon deposits
    B. noisy operation
    C. vapor lock
    D. an explosion

31. The device that operates an oil burner during warm weather, for domestic hot water needs, is the

    A. vaporstat
    B. aquastat
    C. pressuretrol
    D. none of the above

32. The water level in a steam boiler is indicated by the

    A. gauge glass
    B. aquastat
    C. liquid line
    D. all of the above

33. The *stack switch* operates when 33.____

   A. additional hot water is needed
   B. there is an obstruction in the suction line
   C. there is no heat in the smoke stack
   D. all of the above

34. Normal steam pressures in low pressure boilers are below _____ psi. 34.____

   A. 15   B. 25   C. 35   D. 50

35. The *smoke alarm* is mounted on the 35.____

   A. combustion chamber   B. chimney
   C. ignition box   D. none of the above

36. The *pressure gauge* indicates _____ pressure. 36.____

   A. steam   B. water
   C. oil   D. all of the above

37. If excessive pressures are indicated in the steam boiler, you should IMMEDIATELY 37.____

   A. add more water
   B. shut down the oil burner
   C. lower the combustion rate
   D. call the fire department

38. Two devices that work to reduce steam pressure are the _____ and _____. 38.____

   A. vaporstat; pressuretrol
   B. pop off valve; pressuretrol
   C. aquastat; pressuretrol
   D. vaporstat; pop off valve

39. The device that will lock out the oil burner on safety in the presence of excessive steam pressures is the 39.____

   A. safety valve
   B. pressure gauge
   C. manual reset pressuretrol
   D. low water cut off

40. Two conditions that may cause an explosion are _____ and _____. 40.____

   A. afterdrip; dirty rotary cups
   B. ignition failure; afterdrip
   C. ignition failure; excessive steam pressure
   D. leaking oil pump shaft; excessive steam pressure

KEY (CORRECT ANSWERS)

1. A	11. D	21. D	31. B
2. C	12. B	22. A	32. A
3. B	13. A	23. C	33. C
4. A	14. C	24. C	34. A
5. B	15. C	25. A	35. B
6. D	16. B	26. D	36. A
7. B	17. A	27. B	37. B
8. C	18. B	28. C	38. B
9. B	19. D	29. B	39. C
10. C	20. A	30. D	40. C

EXAMINATION SECTION
TEST 1

DIRECTIONS: Each question or incomplete statement is followed by several suggested answers or completions. Select the one that BEST answers the question or completes the statement. *PRINT THE LETTER OF THE CORRECT ANSWER IN THE SPACE AT THE RIGHT.*

1. The MAIN function of a *steam separator* in a steam power plant is to

    A. reduce steam pressure
    B. remove excess oil vapors from the steam
    C. increase steam quality
    D. reduce back-pressure on the steam-driven equipment

2. The MAIN purpose of a *dip tube* in a low-pressure hot water system is to

    A. prevent air from entering the main
    B. determine the level of water in the boiler
    C. reduce air pollution
    D. eliminate condensation when starting up

3. The rating of a unit ventilator is USUALLY determined by a(n)

    A. anemometer   B. hydrometer
    C. psychrometer   D. ammeter

4. Of the following devices, the one that is used to record the air-flow-steam-flow relationship of a boiler in a steam plant is a

    A. Orsat analyzer   B. manometer
    C. steam-flow meter   D. heat meter

5. Of the following types of gas fuels, the one which has the HIGHEST BTU content per cubic foot is _____ gas.

    A. manufactured   B. coke-oven
    C. liquid petroleum   D. natural

6. Of the following gasket materials, the one which is BEST to use when oil at 300° F is being carried in a pipe is

    A. fiber and paper   B. synthetic rubber
    C. asbestos composition   D. corrugated copper

7. A monolithic repair of a slightly damaged sectional magnesia insulation covering is BEST made by

    A. wiring in a *Dutchman* and filling the voids with magnesia cement
    B. covering the damaged area with asbestos laminations
    C. filling in the broken portion with glass-fiber insulating cement
    D. replacing the entire section

8. Of the following piping materials, the one that should NOT be used in a fuel-oil piping system is

   A. galvanized iron
   B. type K copper tubing
   C. brass pipe
   D. steel pipe

9. A valve is marked *300 WOG*.
   This valve could NOT be properly used in a pipe conveying _____ pounds gage maximum.

   A. oil at 300
   B. air at 100
   C. water at 150
   D. steam at 300

10. A steam gage connection for a large boiler is connected to the top of the water column and is then brought down to the operating level 24 feet below. The gage actually reads 605 psi.
    The ACTUAL gage pressure in the boiler is MOST NEARLY _____ psi.

    A. 590   B. 595   C. 610   D. 620

11. Of the following types of industrial oil burners, the one that is COMPLETELY adaptable to fully automatic operation or wide variations in firing rate is the _____ burner.

    A. mechanical-pressure type
    B. air-atomizing
    C. steam-atomizing
    D. horizontal rotary-cup

12. A full backward curve type centrifugal fan is being used in a coal-fired power plant for forced draft. Assume that after adjusting the speed of the fan, it is still too high, resulting in more pressure than is necessary to overcome the resistance of the fuel bed and boiler. To correct this situation, it would be BEST to replace the fan with one of a _____ diameter, running at _____ rpm and with a _____ wheel.

    A. *smaller;* greater; wider
    B. *larger;* less; wider
    C. *larger;* greater; smaller
    D. *smaller;* less; smaller

13. Short stroking in a steam-driven reciprocating pump results in both a(n) _____ in steam consumption and a(n) _____ in pumping capacity.

    A. *decrease;* decrease
    B. *increase;* increase
    C. *decrease;* increase
    D. *increase;* decrease

14. Caustic embrittlement is the weakening of boiler steel as the result of inner crystalline cracks.
    This condition is caused by BOTH long exposure to

    A. a combination of stress and highly acidic water
    B. stress in the presence of free oxygen and highly acidic water
    C. a combination of stress and water with a pH of 7
    D. a combination of stress and highly alkaline water

15. Of the following statements pertaining to feedwater injectors, the one which is MOST nearly correct is that the injectors

    A. are very efficient pumping units
    B. are practical only on small boilers
    C. are very reliable in operation on all types of boilers
    D. can handle 250 to 300 degree water

16. In reference to power plant pumps, the letters N.P.S.H. are an abbreviation for

    A. Non Positive Static Head
    B. Net Position Static Head
    C. Non Positive Standard Head
    D. Net Positive Suction Head

17. A pump's maintenance is based on a preventive maintenance schedule. This means that the schedule should GENERALLY be determined by the

    A. actual time lapse between maintenance checks
    B. actual number of pump-operating hours
    C. pump's actual operating performance
    D. operating performance of the equipment connected to the pump

18. Periodic inspection and testing of mechanical equipment by the staff at a plant is done MAINLY to

    A. help the men to better understand the operation of the equipment
    B. keep the men busy during slack times
    C. encourage the men to better understand each others' working capabilities
    D. discover minor equipment faults before they develop into major breakdowns

19. In planning a preventive maintenance program, the FIRST step to be taken is to

    A. repair all equipment that is not in service
    B. check all fuel oil burner tips
    C. make an inventory of all plant equipment
    D. check all electrical wiring to motors

20. An electric motor having class A insulation has been permitted to operate continuously at rated load even though the internal insulation temperature reads 10C above the allowable maximum internal temperature. Operating at this excessive temperature WOULD

    A. require frequent lubrication of the motor bearings
    B. reduce the life expectancy of the electric motor
    C. require an increase in voltage
    D. reduce the power factor to one-half of its normal value

21. The synchronous speed of a three-phase squirrel cage induction motor operating from a fixed frequency system can ONLY be changed by altering the

    A. rated locked-rotor torque
    B. rheostat position of the unloaded machine
    C. brush holder position
    D. number of poles in the stator

22. A thermal overload relay on an electric motor has been frequently tripping out. Of the following actions, the BEST one to take first to correct this problem would be to

    A. bypass the relay
    B. block the relay on a closed position
    C. clean the relay contacts
    D. arbitrarily readjust the relay setting

23. An air heater for a steam generator providing combustion air at temperatures ranging upward from 300F will often effect savings in fuel ranging from

    A. 1 to 3%   B. 5 to 10%   C. 12 to 15%   D. 17 to 20%

24. You have been asked to make an inspection of the superheater of a steam generator for external corrosion. You should be aware that if the direction of gas flow perpendicular to a tangent to the superheater tube is considered to be the 12 o'clock position, the GREATEST metal loss due to external corrosion usually occurs on the _____ o'clock and _____ o'clock sectors of the tube.

    A. 12; 6   B. 10; 2   C. 8; 3   D. 7; 5

25. In the steam generating plant to which you are assigned, the starting-up time and the shutting-down time for the boiler is determined by the time required to limit the thermal stresses in the drums and headers. The drums and headers have rolled tube joints. The temperature change in saturated temperature per hour for limit controlled heating and cooling rates for this boiler is established at _____ change.

    A. 50° F   B. 75° F   C. 100° F   D. 200° F

KEY (CORRECT ANSWERS)

1. C		11. D	
2. A		12. B	
3. A		13. D	
4. C		14. D	
5. C		15. B	
6. C		16. D	
7. A		17. B	
8. A		18. D	
9. D		19. C	
10. B		20. B	

21. D
22. C
23. B
24. B
25. C

TEST 2

DIRECTIONS: Each question or incomplete statement is followed by several suggested answers or completions. Select the one that BEST answers the question or completes the statement. *PRINT THE LETTER OF THE CORRECT ANSWER IN THE SPACE AT THE RIGHT.*

1. Assume that the optimum pH level of boiler feedwater for a boiler installation ranges between 8.0 and 9.5.
   The alkalizer used in the feedwater treatment to maintain this optimum pH level SHOULD introduce

   A. an average amount of iron and copper corrosion products into the steam cycle
   B. an increase of partial pressure of the carbon dioxide in the steam
   C. the least amount of iron and copper corrosion products into the boiler cycle
   D. a control of corrosion rates by forming a coating on the surfaces contacted by the steam

   1._____

2. The ppm of sodium sulfite that can be *safely* used for the chemical scavenging of oxygen in boiler feedwater is DEPENDENT upon the

   A. steam output of the boiler
   B. boiler operating pressure
   C. number of boiler steam drums
   D. construction of the boiler

   2._____

3. Of the following piping materials, the one which is NOT generally used for pneumatic temperature control systems is

   A. copper   B. plastic
   C. steel   D. galvanized iron

   3._____

4. In accordance with recommended maintenance practice, thermostats used in a pneumatic temperature control system SHOULD be checked

   A. weekly   B. bi-monthly
   C. monthly   D. once a year

   4._____

5. Of the following, the BEST method to use to determine the moisture level in a refrigeration system is to

   A. weigh the drier after it has been in the system for a period of time
   B. visually check the sight glass for particles of corrosion
   C. use a moisture indicator
   D. test a sample of lubricating oil with phosphorus pentoxide

   5._____

6. A full-flow drier is USUALLY recommended to be used in a hermetic refrigeration compressor system to keep the system dry and to

   A. prevent the products of decomposition from getting into the evaporator in the event of a motor burn-out
   B. condense cut liquid refrigerant during compressor off cycles and compressor start-up
   C. prevent the compressor unit from decreasing in capacity
   D. prevent the liquid from dumping into the compressor crankcase

   6._____

7. An economizer in a steam boiler is used to raise the temperature of the
   A. combustion air for firing fuel oil utilizing some of the heat in the exit flue gases
   B. combustion air for firing fuel oil utilizing some of the heat in the exhaust steam from the turbines of steam engines
   C. boiler feedwater by utilizing some of the heat in the exit flue gases
   D. boiler feedwater by utilizing some of the heat in the exhaust steam from the turbines or steam engines

8. A mixed-base grease is a grease that is prepared by mixing lubricating oil with
   A. one metallic soap
   B. two metallic soaps
   C. a synthetic lubricant
   D. heavy gear oil

9. Of the following lubricants, the one which is classified as a circulating oil is _____ oil.
   A. turbine
   B. gear
   C. machine
   D. steam-cylinder

10. You are supervising the installation of a steam-driven reciprocating pump. The pump's air chamber is missing and you have to replace it with one with several salvaged ones. The salvaged air chamber selected should have a volume equal to MOST NEARLY _____ the piston displacement of the pump.
    A. half of
    B. 1 1/2 times
    C. 2 times
    D. 2 1/2 times

11. Economical partial-load operation of steam turbines is obtained by minimizing throttling losses.
    This is accomplished by
    A. reducing the boiler pressure and temperature
    B. throttling the steam flow into the uncontrolled set of nozzles
    C. dividing the first-stage nozzles into several groups and providing a steam control valve for each group
    D. controlling the fuel flow to the steam generator

12. You are ordering two pump wearing rings for a centrifugal pump.
    These rings are GENERALLY identified as
    A. two wearing rings
    B. one drive wearing ring and one casing wearing ring
    C. one casing wearing ring and one impeller wearing ring
    D. one first-stage wearing ring and one drive wearing ring

13. A thermo-hydraulic feedwater regulator is used to regulate the flow of water to a drum-type boiler. The amount of water input to the boiler is controlled *in proportion to* the
    A. boiler load
    B. setting of the feed pump relief valve
    C. amount of water in the outer tube that flashes into steam
    D. water level in the drum

14. The standard capacity rating conditions for any refrigeration compressor is _____ psig for the suction and _____ psig for the discharge.

    A. 5° F, 19.6; 86° F, 154.5
    B. 5° F, 9.6; 96° F, 154.5
    C. 10° F, 9.6; 96° F, 144.5
    D. 10° F, 19.6; 96° F, 134.5

15. Of the following, the MAIN purpose of a subcooler in a refrigerant piping system for a two-stage system is to

    A. reduce the total power requirements and total heat rejection to the second stage
    B. reduce total power requirements and return oil to the compressor
    C. improve the flow of evaporator gas per ton and increase the temperature
    D. increase the heat rejection per ton and avoid system shutdown

16. In large refrigeration systems, the USUAL location for charging the refrigeration system is into the

    A. suction line
    B. liquid line between the receiver shut-off valve and the expansion valve
    C. line between the condenser and the compressor
    D. line between the high pressure cut-off switch and the expansion valve

17. The effect of a voltage variation to 90 percent of normal voltage, for a compound wound DC motor, on the FULL load current is

    A. an increase in the full load current of approximately 10%
    B. a decrease in the full load current of approximately 10%
    C. zero
    D. a decrease in the full load current 20%

18. The purpose of a current-limiting reactor is to place an upper limit on the available short-circuit current that can occur under fault conditions.
    The reactor accomplishes this by contributing _____ to the circuit.

    A. additional capacitance
    B. reduced inductive reactance
    C. reduced capacitance
    D. additional inductive reactance

19. Alternating current electric motors are usually guaranteed to operate satisfactorily and to deliver their full horsepower PROVIDED the electrical power delivered to the motor is at the rated

    A. voltage and at plus or minus 5 percent frequency variation
    B. frequency and at a voltage 15 percent above or below rating
    C. voltage and at plus or minus 10 percent frequency variation
    D. frequency and at a voltage 20 percent above or below rating

20. A three-phase AC motor is connected to a 230 volt, three-phase, alternating current line. With this motor running at full load, the line current is found to be 20 amperes, with a power factor of 0.75.
    Under these conditions, the power, in kilowatts, supplied to this motor will be MOST NEARLY

    A. 3.5
    B. 6.0
    C. 10.5
    D. 18.0

21. In accordance with the air pollution control code, no person shall cause or permit the emission of air contaminants from a boiler with a capacity of 500 million BTU per hour or more, if the air contaminant emitted has a sulfur dioxide content of MORE than _____ parts per million by volume of undiluted emissions measured at _____ percent excess air.

    A. 300; 15　　　B. 200; 10　　　C. 200; 15　　　D. 300; 10

21._____

22. Of the following statements concerning the requirements of the air pollution control code, the one which is the MOST complete and correct is that the owner of equipment

    A. and apparatus shall maintain such equipment and apparatus in good operating order by regular inspection and cleaning and by promptly making repairs
    B. shall maintain the equipment in good operating condition by making inspections and repairs on a regular basis
    C. and apparatus shall maintain the equipment and apparatus in operating condition by regular inspection and cleaning
    D. shall maintain such equipment in good working order by regular inspection and cleaning and by making repairs on a scheduled basis

22._____

23. Assume that one of your assistants was near the Freon 11 refrigeration system when a liquid Freon line ruptured. Some of the liquid Freon 11 has gotten into your assistant's right eye.
    Of the following actions, the one which you should NOT take is to

    A. immediately call for an eye specialist (medical doctor)
    B. gently and quickly rub the Freon 11 out of the eye
    C. use a boric-acid solution to clean out the Freon 11 from his eye
    D. wash the eye by gently blowing the Freon 11 out of his eye with air

23._____

24. Assume that a fire breaks out in an electrical control panel board.
    Of the following types of portable fire extinguishers, the BEST one to use to put out this fire would be a _____ type.

    A. dry-chemical　　　　B. soda-acid
    C. foam　　　　　　　　D. water-stream

24._____

25. Assume that you are checking the water level in a boiler which is on the line in a power plant. Upon opening the gage cocks, you determine that the water level was above the top gage cock.
    Of the following actions, the BEST one to take FIRST in this situation would be to

    A. shut off the fuel and air supply
    B. surface-blow the boiler
    C. close the steam-outlet valve from the boiler
    D. increase the speed of the feedwater pump

25._____

KEY (CORRECT ANSWERS)

1. C
2. B
3. C
4. D
5. C

6. A
7. C
8. B
9. A
10. D

11. C
12. C
13. D
14. A
15. A

16. B
17. A
18. D
19. A
20. B

21. B
22. A
23. B
24. A
25. C

EXAMINATION SECTION
TEST 1

DIRECTIONS: Each question or incomplete statement is followed by several suggested answers or completions. Select the one that BEST answers the question or completes the statement. *PRINT THE LETTER OF THE CORRECT ANSWER IN THE SPACE AT THE RIGHT.*

1. The capacity of a water-cooled condenser is LEAST affected by the

    A. surrounding air temperature
    B. water temperature
    C. refrigerant temperature
    D. quantity of water being circulated

    1._____

2. The type of refrigeration system MOST commonly used in ice-skating rinks is the _____ system.

    A. direct expansion
    B. simple secondary
    C. compound secondary
    D. quadric resistance

    2._____

3. The theoretical amount of refrigeration required to freeze one ton of water from 66° F to ice at 28° F in one day is _____ ton(s).

    A. 1.00   B. 1.25   C. 1.50   D. 1.75

    3._____

4. The brine solution MOST commonly used in ice-skating rink piping, as a freezing medium, is a mixture of water and

    A. calcium chloride
    B. sodium chloride
    C. glycol
    D. methanol

    4._____

5. In an absorption refrigeration system, latent heat is absorbed by the refrigerant in the

    A. evaporator and the generator
    B. evaporator and the absorber
    C. condenser and the absorber
    D. condenser and the generator

    5._____

6. Of the following refrigerants, the one which has the HIGHEST evaporator pressure at the standard 5° F temperature is

    A. ammonia
    B. freon 12
    C. methyl-chloride
    D. carbon dioxide

    6._____

7. The cooler in a refrigeration system that is equipped with automatic protective devices is MOST likely to be accidentally damaged by water freeze-up when the

    A. system is operating under reduced load
    B. system is operating at rated load
    C. system is being pumped down
    D. condenser cooling water flow is interrupted

    7._____

8. The one of the following statements pertaining to refrigerant compressor lubricants that is NOT true is that

   A. the type of oil that is used to lubricate centrifugal compressors can also be used in speed increasers
   B. ammonia causes very little viscosity change in lubricating oil
   C. most reciprocating compressors handling ammonia or freons can be lubricated properly with an oil having a viscosity of 300 Sec. SU @ 100° F
   D. freon 12 causes very little viscosity change in lubricating oil

8.____

9. The one of the following capacity controls which is USUALLY found in a refrigerant reciprocating-compressor system is a

   A. suction valve unloader
   B. throttling damper
   C. variable inlet guide vane
   D. condenser temperature control

9.____

10. A thermostatic expansion valve is connected to an evaporator operating at 5° F and 11.8 psig. The valve is in equilibrium at 10° superheat, and the pressure in the bulb is 17.7 psig.
    The EQUIVALENT valve-spring pressure on the refrigerant side of the sensitive element is _____ psi.

    A. 5.9   B. 10.9   C. 22.8   D. 29.5

10.____

11. A pressure gage on a compressed air tank reads 35.3 psi at 70° F.
    If, due to a fire, the temperature of the air in the tank were to increase to 600° F, the gage reading should be MOST NEARLY _____ psi.

    A. 70   B. 75   C. 80   D. 85

11.____

12. An ADVANTAGE that variable-speed control of a fan has over damper control is

    A. lower first-cost of controls
    B. lower power consumption
    C. cheaper fan drive motor
    D. constant high efficiency throughout entire fan load range

12.____

13. An intercooler is used on a two-stage air compressor to reduce the

    A. cylinder temperature in the first stage
    B. amount of condensate in the second stage
    C. back pressure of the air in the first stage
    D. work done on the air in the second stage

13.____

14. Of the following, the BEST instrument to use to measure small pressure differentials at low pressure is the

    A. mercury manometer   B. bourdon tube gage
    C. pressurtrol   D. inclined manometer

14.____

15. A modulating pressurtrol on a boiler should contain a

   A. potentiometer
   B. mercury switch
   C. manual reset lever
   D. level indicator

16. Of the following automatic refrigerant expansion valves, the one which can only be used in a system where the liquid refrigerant can largely be stored in the evaporator without danger of sending slugs of liquid refrigerant over to the compressor is the _____ valve.

   A. thermal-expansion
   B. diaphragm-expansion
   C. high-side float
   D. low-side float

17. The refrigerating effect of a fluid is measured by the amount of heat it is capable of absorbing from the time it enters the

   A. evaporator as a liquid and leaves as a vapor
   B. condenser as a vapor and leaves as a liquid
   C. expansion valve as a liquid and leaves as a vapor
   D. compressor as a vapor and leaves as a vapor

18. The one of the following which lists the refrigerants in CORRECT order of decreasing toxicity is:

   A. Ammonia, sulphur dioxide, freon 12
   B. Sulphur dioxide, ammonia, freon 12
   C. Sulphur dioxide, freon 12, ammonia
   D. Ammonia, freon 12, sulphur dioxide

19. The one of the following methods which would MOST likely be used to control the capacity of a large centrifugal refrigerant compressor is the _____ method.

   A. cylinder unloader
   B. variable cylinder clearance
   C. variable speed
   D. stop and start

20. On a hot summer day, the GREATEST number of people working in a large air-conditioned office would feel comfortable if the temperature and relative humidity were maintained at

   A. 77° F and 50%
   B. 80° F and 60%
   C. 74° F and 30%
   D. 71° F and 50%

21. The one of the following conditions which has the GREATEST effect on the suction pressure on a swimming pool circulating pump is a

   A. clogged hair and lint strainer
   B. loss of coagulant
   C. low pH level
   D. clogged filter

22. A coagulant used in swimming pool filters is

   A. alum
   B. chlorine
   C. soda-ash
   D. sodium hypochlorite

23. According to the health code, the pH reading of swimming pool water should be between _____ and _____.

    A. 5.8; 6.4 B. 6.8; 7.4 C. 7.8; 8.4 D. 8.8; 9.4

24. An orthotolidine test is made to find out how much of which substance is contained in a sample of water?

    A. Alum B. Ammonia C. Chlorine D. Soda-ash

25. The MINIMUM air temperature which must be maintained in an indoor swimming pool, except during the summer months, is _____ °F.

    A. 68 B. 71 C. 75 D. 82

KEY (CORRECT ANSWERS)

1. A
2. B
3. B
4. A
5. A

6. D
7. C
8. D
9. A
10. A

11. D
12. B
13. D
14. D
15. A

16. C
17. A
18. B
19. C
20. A

21. A
22. A
23. C
24. C
25. C

TEST 2

DIRECTIONS: Each question or incomplete statement is followed by several suggested answers or completions. Select the one that BEST answers the question or completes the statement. *PRINT THE LETTER OF THE CORRECT ANSWER IN THE SPACE AT THE RIGHT.*

1. A permit is required for the storage or use of liquid chlorine.   1.____
 This permit is issued by which city agency?
 The

 A. Health Services Administration
 B. Board of Standards and Appeals
 C. Board of Water Supply
 D. Fire Department

2. The MINIMUM amount of free chlorine that swimming pool water should contain for   2.____
 proper disinfection is _____ part(s) per million.

 A. 1.0   B. 10   C. 40   D. 400

3. The agency which approves gas masks suitable for use in high concentrations of chlo-   3.____
 rine gas is the United States

 A. Environmental Protection Agency
 B. Department of Agriculture
 C. Bureau of Mines
 D. Department of Defense

4. The daily operational records of swimming pools which are required by the health code   4.____
 must be kept for a period of AT LEAST

 A. one month   B. six months
 C. one year   D. two years

5. The one of the following which is NOT used as a filtering media in swimming pool filters   5.____
 is

 A. sand   B. quartz
 C. diatomaceous earth   D. clay

6. The point at which swimming pool filters should be back-washed is when the difference   6.____
 between the inlet and outlet pressure EXCEEDS _____ psi.

 A. 5   B. 10   C. 15   D. 20

7. Of the following valves, the type which can be used to adjust the rate-of-flow in a swim-   7.____
 ming pool filter is the _____ valve.

 A. butterfly   B. needle
 C. gate   D. stop-and-waste

8. When the coagulant in a swimming pool filter fails to jelly, the MOST likely cause of the   8.____
 failure is

 A. high water temperature   B. excess bacteria in the water
 C. insufficient alkalinity of the water   D. excess algae in the water

9. Of the following types of flow meters, the one that is MOST accurate is a

   A. concentric orifice
   B. venturi tube
   C. flow nozzle
   D. pitot tube

10. A spring pop safety valve on a fired high-pressure boiler fails to pop at its set pressure. Which of the following methods should be used to free the valve before retesting it?

    A. Strike the valve body with a soft lead hammer until it pops
    B. Raise the valve lifting-lever and release it
    C. Reduce the spring compression gradually until the valve opens
    D. Unscrew the valve one-quarter turn to relieve the strain on it

11. A device which retains the desired parts of a steam and water mixture while rejecting the undesired parts of the mixture is a

    A. check valve
    B. calorimeter
    C. stud tube
    D. steam trap

12. The PRIMARY purpose of using phosphate to treat boiler water is to

    A. precipitate the hardness constituents
    B. scavenge the dissolved oxygen
    C. dissolve the calcium
    D. dissolve the magnesium

13. The efficiency of a riveted joint is defined as the ratio of the

    A. plate thickness to the rivet diameter
    B. strength of the riveted joint to the strength of a welded joint
    C. strength of the riveted joint to the strength of the solid plate
    D. number of rivets in the first row of the joint to the total number of rivets on one side of the joint

14. A pump delivers 1500 pounds of water per minute against a total head of 200 feet. The water horsepower of this pump is MOST NEARLY

    A. 10
    B. 40
    C. 100
    D. 600

15. A centrifugal water pump is direct-driven by a 25 HP 900 RPM electric motor at rated load.
    In order to double the quantity of water delivered, it would be necessary to substitute a motor rated at _____ HP at _____ RPM.

    A. 40; 1200
    B. 50; 1200
    C. 100; 1800
    D. 200; 1800

16. Of the following fire extinguisher ratings, the one which indicates that an extinguisher has the GREATEST capability for extinguishing wood, paper, and electrical fires is

    A. 2-A:16-B:C
    B. 4-A:4-B:C
    C. 16-A
    D. 8-B

17. Of the following combinations of oil burners and fuel oils, the combination which is the MOST hazardous to fire-up when placing a cold boiler into service is the

    A. compressed air-atomized burner firing light oil
    B. steam-atomized burner firing heavy oil
    C. air-atomized burner firing heavy oil
    D. mechanically-atomized burner firing heavy oil

18. It is usually desirable to have a program which will create and maintain the interest of workers in safety. Of the following, the one which such a program CANNOT do is to

    A. develop safe work habits
    B. compensate for unsafe procedures
    C. provide a channel of communications between workers and management
    D. give employees a chance to participate in accident prevention activities

19. Because of a ruptured ammonia tank, the concentration of ammonia gas in a room exceeds 3%.
    The wearing of a gas mask, as the only protective device, by a person entering the room is

    A. *recommended,* because the gas mask alone is sufficient protection
    B. *not recommended,* because the ammonia will severely irritate the skin
    C. *not recommended,* because the gas mask is not effective at concentrations above 3%
    D. *not recommended,* because ammonia is flammable

20. The Occupational Safety and Health Act of 1970 provided for

    A. penalties against employees for safety violations
    B. complete occupational safety against all hazards
    C. standards of employee discipline
    D. employees' right to review a copy of a safety citation against the employer

21. An aftercooler on a reciprocating air compressor is used PRIMARILY to

    A. increase compressor capacity
    B. improve compressor efficiency
    C. condense the moisture in the compressed air
    D. cool the lubricating oil

22. The one of the following tasks which is an example of preventive maintenance is

    A. replacing a leaking water pipe nipple
    B. cleaning the cup on a rotary cup burner
    C. cleaning a completely clogged oil strainer
    D. replacing a blown fuse

23. The four MAIN causes of failure of three-phase electric motors are

    A. dirt, friction, moisture, single-phasing
    B. friction, moisture, single-phasing, vibration
    C. dirt, moisture, single-phasing, vibration
    D. dirt, friction, moisture, vibration

24. The one of the following electrical control components that may be lubricated is the

    A. drum controller's copper-to-copper contacts
    B. relay bearing
    C. starter silver contact
    D. shunt spring

25. In the planning of a preventive maintenance program, the FIRST requirement is to

    A. prepare a maintenance manual
    B. inventory the equipment
    C. inventory the tools available
    D. prepare repair requisitions for all equipment not operating satisfactorily

KEY (CORRECT ANSWERS)

1. D		11. D	
2. A		12. A	
3. C		13. C	
4. B		14. A	
5. D		15. D	
6. B		16. B	
7. A		17. D	
8. C		18. B	
9. B		19. B	
10. B		20. D	

21. C
22. B
23. D
24. A
25. B

EXAMINATION SECTION
TEST 1

DIRECTIONS: Each question or incomplete statement is followed by several suggested answers or completions. Select the one that BEST answers the question or completes the statement. *PRINT THE LETTER OF THE CORRECT ANSWER IN THE SPACE AT THE RIGHT.*

1. Which type of vertical fire tube boiler generates the driest steam?

    A. Exposed tube
    B. Submerged tube
    C. "Dry back"
    D. All of the above

2. The vertically inclined type water tube boiler(s) is (are) manufactured by

    A. Stirling
    B. Combustion Engineering Co.
    C. Foster-Wheeler
    D. all of the above

3. Which of the following statements, pertaining to high pressure, high temperature, forced hot water circulation systems, is CORRECT?

    A. One cubic foot of water carries 56.6 times as much heat as one cubic foot of steam
    B. A HPHT water system cannot be used to make steam for process services
    C. Conventional type boilers cannot be used for HPHT water systems
    D. All of the above

4. Upon entering the boiler room, you find the water out of the glass, the safety valve blowing off strong, and a fire under the boiler.
Your FIRST action would be to

    A. remove the fire with draft and damper open
    B. cool the boiler down completely
    C. prevent priming by not raising the safety valve or making change in operation of engines or boiler
    D. all of the above

5. The A.S.M.E. Boiler Code for boiler shells requires a tensile strength of _____ lbs. per sq. in.

    A. 10,000 to 20,000
    B. 25,000 to 45,000
    C. 55,000 to 63,000
    D. 70,000 to 85,000

6. The BEST time to blow a boiler down is

    A. once a day when the load is lightest
    B. once a day under full load
    C. when the chemical concentration is greatest
    D. once a shift

7. What is the horsepower of a boiler 42 inches in diameter and 18 feet long, with two 12 inch flues?

    A. 100
    B. 50.5
    C. 21.2
    D. 15

8. The safety valve should be *large* enough to

   A. discharge all of the steam the boiler can generate when operated at peak capacity
   B. expel the steam above the working pressure of the boiler
   C. discharge the steam above the bursting pressure of the boiler
   D. all of the above

9. If a boiler has 500 sq. ft. or more of heating surface and the steam generating capacity is 2,000 lbs. of water per hour, or more

   A. a 4 inch safety valve is required
   B. a A.S.M.E. approved pop safety valve is required
   C. two or more safety valves are required
   D. it must be inspected every month

10. A superheater

    A. *increases* the efficiency of a boiler
    B. *decreases* the efficiency of a boiler
    C. *increases* the efficiency of engines and turbines
    D. raises the temperature precipitously

11. For satisfactory burning of oil, burners must atomize the oil by using

    A. jets of steam or air
    B. high oil pressure
    C. a rotating cup operating at high speed
    D. all of the above

12. The chief cause(s) of excessive stoker furnace maintenance is(are)

    A. excessive overloading the stoker and carrying very high ratings
    B. badly clinkering coal combined with widely swinging loads, resulting in blocking the air flow through some part and consistent overheating of the stoker parts
    C. the ash content of the coal being too low, bringing the burning fuel in direct contact with the grate
    D. all of the above

13. Draft is measured in

    A. pounds per square inch
    B. inches of vacuum
    C. inches of water
    D. foot lbs.

14. "Balanced draft" pressure

    A. in the furnace is approximately that of the outside atmosphere
    B. in the flue gas system is constant throughout
    C. measures between 0.15 to 0.3 inches of water column
    D. cannot be measured accurately

15. Forced draft is produced by

A. the difference in density of a column of heated air and the density of the cooler surrounding atmosphere
B. a fan or blower which forces the air into the furnace at a pressure above that of the atmosphere
C. a fan located between the boiler and the stack
D. changes in pressure that occur naturally

16. A duplex compound engine has

    A. its two cylinders along a common axis or line
    B. two tandem conpound cylinders which are parallel and adjacent to each other
    C. two parallel cylinders on the same side of the crank shaft, each piston being connected by a separate connecting rod to the one crank shaft
    D. none of the above

17. The engine that has four valves which oscillate with two valves located in each end of the cylinder with one for admitting steam, and the other for exhausting is a _____ valve engine.

    A. simple slide   B. Corliss
    C. double ported   D. reciprocating steam

18. A safety stop is used on fly ball governors to prevent the

    A. belt driving the governor from ripping
    B. driving gears from becoming disengaged
    C. governor balls from flying out with an increase of speed
    D. bearings from dislocating

19. *Hunting* of a shaft governor is caused by

    A. too much friction
    B. weak springs
    C. very close regulation with a free moving governo
    D. all of the above

20. A divergent nozzle used in a steam turbine is used when the

    A. throat of the nozzle is smaller than the mouth
    B. throat is of the same or larger cross sectional area than the mouth of the nozzle
    C. mouth and throat of the nozzle are the same size
    D. throat of the nozzle is of the same size as the mouth

21. An impulse turbine depends upon _____ percentage of impulsive force for its operation.

    A. 100   B. 90   C. 80   D. 70

22. Leakage between the shaft and diaphragm which separates the rows of moving blades is *prevented* by

    A. packing
    B. nitrogen seals
    C. a labyrinth passageway or carbon seals
    D. all of the above

23. Reaction turbines are *usually* designed for operating on

    A. low pressure and exhausting into the atmosphere
    B. low pressure and exhausting into a condenser
    C. high pressure and exhausting into a condenser
    D. all of the above

24. Steam turbine reduction gears are classified as _____ gears.

    A. single reduction
    B. double reduction
    C. epicyclis
    D. all of the above

25. The principle cause of turbine vibrations is (are)

    A. poor alignment and poor foundation
    B. loose parts, internal rubbing, and scale deposits on blading
    C. out of balance due to worn or broken blades
    D. all of the above

26. The maximum oil temperature allowed in the main bearings is

    A. 100° F.
    B. 250° F.
    C. 325° F.
    D. all of the above

27. The critical speed of a turbine shaft is the speed

    A. at which the shaft vibrates most violently
    B. that is below the operating speed
    C. that is above the operating speed
    D. at which vibration stops

28. The types of condensers used with steam engines and turbines are:
    I. Barometric
    II. Surface
    III. Jet condenser
    IV. Reciprocating

    The CORRECT answer is:

    A. I, II *only*
    B. I, II, III
    C. II, III *only*
    D. II, III, IV

29. The pumps used for removing non-condensable gases from the condenser are:
    I. Wet air pump
    II. Dry air pump
    III. Steam jet air pump
    IV. Rotary

    The correct answer is:

    A. I, II *only*
    B. II, III *only*
    C. I, II, III
    D. II, III, IV

30. The types of pumps MOST commonly used for circulating water in a condenser system are:
    I. Centrifugal
    II. Reciprocating
    III. Rotary
    IV. Steamjet

    The CORRECT answer is:

    A. I, II only
    B. I, II, III
    C. II, III only
    D. II, III, IV

KEY (CORRECT ANSWERS)

1.	A	16.	D
2.	D	17.	B
3.	D	18.	A
4.	A	19.	D
5.	C	20.	A
6.	C	21.	A
7.	C	22.	D
8.	A	23.	D
9.	C	24.	D
10.	C	25.	D
11.	D	26.	C
12.	D	27.	A
13.	C	28.	B
14.	C	29.	C
15.	B	30.	B

TEST 2

DIRECTIONS: Each question or incomplete statement is followed by several suggested answers or completions. Select the one that BEST answers the question or completes the statement. *PRINT THE LETTER OF THE CORRECT ANSWER IN THE SPACE AT THE RIGHT.*

1. Which operations are performed in starting a duplex pump?
   I. Open the valves in exhaust steam line, open the drain cocks
   II. Open suction valve on water end and also delivery valve
   III. Start pump slowly, close drains, gradually increase speed until desired strokes are obtained
   IV. Crack the steam valve allowing condensate to blow through the drain cocks
   The CORRECT answer is:

   A. I, II, III
   B. II, III, IV
   C. I, III, IV
   D. I, II, III, IV

   1.____

2. Which conditions may cause a pump to fail to raise water?
   I. Worn or broken valve
   II. Pump needs priming or pump is air or gas bound
   III. Air leaks around the suction pipe
   IV. Leakage of suction valves
   The CORRECT answer is:

   A. I, II, III
   B. II, III, IV
   C. I, II, IV
   D. I, II, III, IV

   2.____

3. A CO meter tells when there is

   A. excess air
   B. complete combustion
   C. excess carbon dioxide
   D. danger

   3.____

4. A steam engine indicator diagram

   A. calculates the horsepower and the steam consumption of an engine
   B. sets the valves of an engine
   C. detects the cause of many operation troubles
   D. all of the above

   4.____

5. The type of valve BEST suited for steam throttling is the

   A. globe
   B. gate
   C. needle
   D. all of the above

   5.____

6. The danger from using a low flash point oil in air compressors is that

   A. the oil will not lubricate the cylinder walls
   B. excessive moisture is formed
   C. explosion in the air compressor, receiver or piping is possible
   D. the compressor will seize

   6.____

7. It is evident that there is sufficient water going to the cylinder jackets by the temperature of the

   A. air leaving the compressor
   B. jacket water leaving the compressor
   C. air leaving the intercooler
   D. all of the above

8. The unit used to indicate the quantity of heat is

   A. degrees Fahrenheit
   B. degrees centigrade
   C. B.t.u.
   D. all of the above

9. The function of the expansion valve in a refrigerating system is to

   A. control or meter the liquid flow to the expansion coils or evaporator
   B. regulate the gas flow to the expansion coils or evaporator
   C. control the temperature in the expansion coils or evaporator
   D. all of the above

10. The capacity of a compressor is determined by the

    A. weight of the refrigerant pumped
    B. temperature of the evaporator and condenser
    C. volumetric efficiency of the compressor
    D. pressure of the evaporator and condenser

11. The condenser requiring the MOST cooling surface is the _____ type.

    A. shell and tube
    B. submerged
    C. atmospheric or surface
    D. all of the above

12. The presence of a non-condensable gas in the condenser affects the transmission of heat between the water and refrigerant by

    A. displacing the refrigerant
    B. acting as an insulation and reducing the heat transfer
    C. reducing the capacity of the condenser
    D. all of the above

13. Frost on cooling coils

    A. *raises* the boiling point of the refrigerant
    B. *decreases* the suction pressure
    C. *increases* the suction pressure
    D. none of the above

14. Humidity is important in cold storage rooms in order to

    A. prevent shrinkage and drying
    B. lower the temperature
    C. increase formation of frost
    D. all of the above

15. For MAXIMUM capacity and efficiency

    A. the condenser pressure and the suction pressure should be nearly the same
    B. the suction pressure should be as high as practicable
    C. the discharge pressure should be as low as practicable
    D. all of the above

16. The unit used to measure the time rate of flow of a quantity of electricity is the

    A. watt   B. ampere   C. coulomb   D. ohm

17. The volt is the unit used to measure

    A. power   B. resistance
    C. potential difference   D. all of the above

18. Ohm's law states that the current varies

    A. *directly* as the potential difference, and *inversely* as the resistance
    B. *inversely* as the potential difference, and *diversely* as the resistance
    C. *directly* as the potential difference and *directly* as the resistance
    D. none of the above

19. House lights are connected in parallel instead of series because

    A. the voltage must be the same across each lamp
    B. fewer amperes of current will flow through each lamp
    C. the current passing through one lamp will pass through each of the other lamps
    D. all of the above

20. A watt is equal to

    A. ohm x volt   B. amp x volt
    C. ohm x amp   D. coulomb ÷ volt

21. If coil A has 50 turns of wire and coil B has 200, whenever a current is induced in the right circuit the

    A. electric power in coil B will be about the same as that in coil A
    B. voltage in coil A will be 4 times that in coil B
    C. current in coil A will be about 1/4 that in coil B
    D. all of the above

22. In the induction motor

    A. current is fed into the rotor by brushes and a commutator
    B. the rotor is not connected to the A.C. supply
    C. the speed of the rotor is equal to that of the revolving magnetic field
    D. none of the above

23. A 60-cycle, single phase motor draws 7.5 amperes at 120 volts and has an inductive power factor of 85% at this load.
    How much power, in watts, is the motor using?

    A. 525   B. 655
    C. 765   D. None of the above

24. A 60-pole alternator turns at 100 RPM. 24.____
What is the frequency, in cycles of the a-c produced?

    A. 30   B. 50   C. 60   D. 75

25. A circuit containing *only* resistance and inductance in series, is connected to a 120 volt 60-cycle line. 25.____
The current will

    A. increase   B. lag behind the emf
    C. be in phase with the emf   D. all of the above

26. What is the safe working pressure, in pounds, of a boiler with a 5/8 inch plate, 60,000 lb. tensile strength, 60 inch diameter and triple reveted joints, using a factor of safety of 5? 26.____

Use the formula: Safe working pressure $= \dfrac{2 \times S \times T \times E}{F \times T}$

    A. 115   B. 185.5
    C. 217.5   D. none of the above

27. What is the mechanical efficiency of an engine which delivers 200 brake H.P. while showing 250 indicated H.P.? Use the formula: Mechanical efficiency $= \dfrac{\text{Brake H.P.}}{\text{Indicated H.P.}}$ 27.____

    A. 80%   B. 90%   C. 95%   D. 100%

28. A pump delivers 500 cubic feet of water per minute and the pump displacement is 560 cubic feet. 28.____
What is the slip?

Use the formula: Slip $= \dfrac{\text{Slip}}{\text{Displacement}}$

    A. 10.7%   B. 15.5%   C. 18.7%   D. 21.3%

29. A boiler is operating under 120 psi absolute pressure with feedwater at 160°F. The factor of evaporation is 1.063.5/970.4 = 1.097 29.____
If the total evaporation is 8,760 lb/hr. what boiler horsepower is the boiler developing?

Use the formula: Boiler H.P. $= \dfrac{\text{Total Evaporation} \times \text{Factor Of Evaporation}}{34.5}$

    A. 300   B. 278   C. 236   D. 212

30. If an ammonia system was working at 15 lb. gage suction pressure and the temperature of liquid ammonia entering the evaporator through the expansion valve was 90 degrees, how many B.t.u. per lb. would be available for useful work, assuming that the total heat of 1 lb. of ammonia at 15 lb. gage pressure is 611.4 B.t.u., and the heat of the liquid at 90 degrees F. is 143.5 B.t.u.? 30.____

    A. 376.5   B. 422.7   C. 467.9   D. 494.8

KEY (CORRECT ANSWERS)

1.	D	16.	C
2.	D	17.	C
3.	B	18.	A
4.	D	19.	A
5.	C	20.	B
6.	C	21.	C
7.	D	22.	B
8.	C	23.	D
9.	D	24.	B
10.	C	25.	C
11.	C	26.	D
12.	D	27.	A
13.	D	28.	A
14.	A	29.	B
15.	D	30.	C

EXAMINATION SECTION
TEST 1

DIRECTIONS: Each question or incomplete statement is followed by several suggested answers or completions. Select the one that BEST answers the question or completes the statement. *PRINT THE LETTER OF THE CORRECT ANSWER IN THE SPACE AT THE RIGHT.*

1. A(n) _____ pump is used to transfer fuel oil. 1._____

    A. gear
    B. injector
    C. centrifugal
    D. reciprocating

2. A fuel oil tank is located above the pump. A siphon should be located between the 2._____

    A. preheater and pump
    B. pump and boiler
    C. tank and pump
    D. tank and aquastat

3. *WOG* stands for 3._____

    A. water or gas
    B. water, oil, gas
    C. water, gas, steam
    D. all of the above

4. The _____ pump is NOT a positive displacement pump. 4._____

    A. gear
    B. centrifugal
    C. screw
    D. reciprocating

5. An unloader is used on an air compressor to 5._____

    A. start easier
    B. stop easier
    C. run faster
    D. none of the above

6. An intercooler is associated with a(n) 6._____

    A. air compressor
    B. steam engine
    C. feedwater heater
    D. condenser

7. What is added to oil to prevent sludge or lacquer from forming? 7._____

    A. Detergents
    B. Anti-foaming agents
    C. Inhibitors
    D. Phosphates

8. Greatest wear occurs on a steam turbine between the moving and stationary parts 8._____

    A. at 20% over normal speed
    B. at 10% over normal speed
    C. at normal speed
    D. below normal speed

9. A *gag* is USUALLY put on a safety prior to 9._____

    A. external inspection
    B. internal inspection
    C. hydrostatic inspection
    D. removing hand holes

10. To calibrate a steam gauge, you use a 10._____

    A. dead weight tester
    B. fyrite instrument
    C. spring scale lifter
    D. pyrometer

11. When not more than two safety valves of different sizes are used, the relieving capacity of the smaller valve shall NOT be less than _____ % of the larger valve.

    A. 20   B. 30   C. 40   D. 50

12. *Blow off* piping USUALLY refers to

    A. piping at the lowest part of the boiler
    B. piping coming from the safeties
    C. piping coming from the superheater
    D. vent pipes

13. The heating value of coal is 14,000 BTU per pound. It is necessary to produce 1,400,000 BTU per hour.
    If a boiler has a 60% efficiency rate, how many pounds must be burned?

    A. 60   B. 170   C. 225   D. 100

14. You are working the 4:00 P.M. to Midnight shift at an energy producing, coal burning steam plant.
    The FIRST thing you would do when coming to work is

    A. add green coal and build up the fire
    B. blow down gauge glass and determine water level
    C. clean the fires
    D. blow down the boiler

15. On a 3" safety valve set to blow at 300 psi, what is the pressure needed to lift it?

    A. 2120   B. 300   C. 3000   D. 2425

16. On a horizontal return tubular boiler, there is a baffle located near the exit of the boiler. Its purpose is to provide _____ steam.

    A. wet   B. dry
    C. superheated   D. saturated

17. Most high temperature, high pressure boilers have high evaporative rates.
    Because of this,

    A. water must be treated so that scale does not form on the inside of the tubes
    B. it maintains proper water levels
    C. it operates efficiently
    D. it works better with no returns

18. Soot is formed on a water tube boiler

    A. on the fan blades of the forced draft fan
    B. on the inside of the tubes
    C. on the outside of the tubes
    D. in the steam drum

19. In order to make a tight joint between a tube and a tube sheet, 19.____

   A. use a self-feeding tube expander
   B. use a ball-peen hammer and a blunt cold chisel
   C. weld in place
   D. heat will expand the tubes

20. Give external heating area in square feet of tube with the following dimensions: tube interior diameter, 5 inches; wall thickness, 1/2 inch and 18 feet long. 20.____

   A. 19.25   B. 24.25   C. 26.50   D. 28.26

21. Give external heating area in square feet of 100 tubes 3 1/2 inches external diameter, 12 feet long. 21.____

   A. 1100   B. 1200   C. 1300   D. 1400

22. A safety valve capacity must be such that it can discharge all the steam that a boiler can generate without rising more than _____% above the highest pressure at which any safety valve is set. 22.____

   A. 3   B. 6   C. 7   D. 8

23. The depth of the fuel bed on a chain grate stoker is controlled by a 23.____

   A. guillotine or knife gate
   B. height of ignition arch
   C. speed of stoker drive or air pressure
   D. size of grates

24. Tuyeres are used to provide air for 24.____

   A. an underfed stoker   B. a sprinkler stoker
   C. a rotary cup burner   D. steam atomizing burners

25. A pulverized boiler has the GREATEST danger of explosion when it has a _____ rate of fire. 25.____

   A. low   B. 70%   C. 100%   D. 110%

KEY (CORRECT ANSWERS)

1. A
2. C
3. B
4. B
5. A

6. A
7. A
8. D
9. C
10. A

11. D
12. A
13. B
14. B
15. A

16. B
17. A
18. C
19. A
20. D

21. A
22. B
23. A
24. A
25. A

TEST 2

DIRECTIONS: Each question or incomplete statement is followed by several suggested answers or completions. Select the one that BEST answers the question or completes the statement. *PRINT THE LETTER OF THE CORRECT ANSWER IN THE SPACE AT THE RIGHT.*

1. Draft is measured in

    A. pounds per square inch
    B. inches of mercury
    C. feet of water
    D. inches of water

    1.____

2. In a natural draft boiler, a _____ is used to prevent excess draft from occurring.

    A. siphon
    B. stack switch
    C. barometric damper
    D. all of the above

    2.____

3. Approximate analysis would include

    A. fixed carbon, moisture, and ash
    B. sulphur, volatile matter, and moisture
    C. ash, moisture, volatile matter, and fixed carbon,
    D. fixed carbon, ash, and volatile matter

    3.____

4. What is considered good combustion in an oil-fired boiler? _____% CO_2.

    A. 8   B. 10   C. 12   D. 14

    4.____

5. In an oil-fired boiler, the flue gas analysis indicates 10.5% CO_2. This would indicate an excess air of MOST NEARLY

    A. 30%   B. 40%   C. 60%   D. 70%

    5.____

6. In terms of environmental pollution, the three elements which are MOST damaging are

    A. carbon monoxide, sulphur, and particulate matter
    B. carbon dioxide, sulphur, and oxygen
    C. particulate matter, sulphur, and carbon dioxide
    D. oxygen and sulphur

    6.____

7. A rotary cup burner is easy to distinguish because it has a(n)

    A. oil line and steam line
    B. high pressure air line and low pressure air line
    C. oil line and centrifugal fan
    D. oil line, air line, and steam line

    7.____

8. What type of fire extinguisher would be used on a *live* electrical wire?

    A. Soda foam
    B. Water
    C. Carbon dioxide
    D. Halon

    8.____

9. Fuel oil is heated in a storage tank by use of

    A. fuel oil burner
    B. steam
    C. hot air
    D. electric coils

    9.____

10. The LOWEST point at which fuel oil will flow under standard conditions is known as

   A. viscosity point B. flashpoint
   C. pour point D. specific gravity

11. What lubrication would you NOT use when the temperature was 160°?

   A. Calcium B. Sodium C. Lithium D. Aluminum

12. To lubricate the piston on the water end of a duplex pump, you would use

   A. water B. oil C. grease D. graphite

13. To oil multiple bearings in an enclosed space, use a

   A. ring or chain oiler B. drip
   C. splash D. capillary

14. A new boiler is erected and the main supports are from the roof.
    An advantage of this method is

   A. to relieve pressure at the bottom of the boiler
   B. to allow for expansion
   C. it is easier to build
   D. it is less expensive

15. How many cubic feet are there in a coal bin that is 24 feet long and 20 feet wide if the front of the bin is 4 feet high and the rear of the bin is 12 feet high?

   A. 4000 B. 6000 C. 2000 D. 8000

16. The purpose of a feedwater heater used with a boiler is to heat

   A. and treat water used in the boiler
   B. the fuel oil
   C. the steam
   D. the intake air

17. On a d-slide valve engine, lengthening the valve stem causes earlier

   A. crank-end admission B. head-end admission
   C. crank-end cutoff D. head-end compression

18. The dimensions of a pump are 18 x 16 x 24. What does 16 stand for?

   A. Steam end B. Water end
   C. Valve stem length D. Steam flow

19. A centrifugal pump makes more noise as the rate of water pressure increases.
    The reason for this is

   A. specific gravity of water
   B. cavitation
   C. the water is too hot
   D. none of the above

20. Which of the following is NOT a positive displacement pump?

   A. Screw type B. Reciprocating C. Gear type D. Centrifugal

21. An injector is the same as a(n)   21.____

    A. ejector
    B. boiler feed pump
    C. tank
    D. blow down tank

22. A closed feedwater heater has steam   22.____

    A. going through the feedwater heater
    B. and water mixing directly
    C. and water not in direct contact
    D. and air mixing together

23. M.E.P. stands for   23.____

    A. minimum exhaust pressure
    B. maximum efficiency point
    C. mean effective pressure
    D. maximum exhaust pressure

24. The MAIN function of the steam jacket in a steam engine is to   24.____

    A. *reduce* initial condensation in the cylinders
    B. *decrease* the superheat of the steam going to the cylinders
    C. *increase* the expansion of steam in the cylinders
    D. *decrease* the speed of the engine

25. In a noncondensing steam engine, the compounding reduces the steam consumption by   25.____

    A. 5% to 10%   B. 10 to 25%   C. 25 to 40%   D. 40 to 50%

KEY (CORRECT ANSWERS)

1. D		11. D	
2. C		12. A	
3. C		13. A	
4. C		14. B	
5. B		15. A	
6. A		16. A	
7. C		17. A	
8. C		18. B	
9. B		19. D	
10. C		20. D	

21. B
22. C
23. C
24. A
25. C

TEST 3

DIRECTIONS: Each question or incomplete statement is followed by several suggested answers or completions. Select the one that BEST answers the question or completes the statement. *PRINT THE LETTER OF THE CORRECT ANSWER IN THE SPACE AT THE RIGHT.*

1. The steam rate on a steam engine can be expressed as

    A. degrees Fahrenheit
    B. per pound of fuel burned
    C. pounds per hour
    D. gallons of water

    1._____

2. In a steam generating plant operating condensing, if a deaerating heater is used, it would be located between the

    A. boiler and condenser on the feedwater line
    B. boiler and the condenser on the exhaust line
    C. engine and the condenser on the exhaust line
    D. engine and the condenser on the main steam line

    2._____

3. A manufacturing plant is equipped with a bleeder turbine with the bleed steam used for the purpose of processing. When the demand for process steam falls off, the bled steam is

    A. exhausted into the atmosphere
    B. put into the heating system
    C. used in the lower pressure stages of the turbine
    D. all of the above

    3._____

4. A turbine generator at full load runs at 1765 RPM. At no load, it runs at 1800 RPM. Its speed regulation is MOST NEARLY

    A. 2%   B. 3%   C. 5%   D. 10%

    4._____

5. _____ are NOT used to seal the steam space of a turbine.

    A. Labyrinth seals   B. Carbon packing rings
    C. Water glands   D. Oil seals

    5._____

6. A motor with a large starting torque is a _____ motor.

    A. squirrel cage induction   B. synchronous
    C. shunt wound   D. wound induction

    6._____

7. What is the horsepower of an engine having an 8 x 12 cylinder, mean effective pressure of 90, and an RPM of 330?

    A. 50   B. 90   C. 100   D. 190

    7._____

8. You get oil out of boiler feedwater by

    A. deionization   B. coagulation
    C. lime-soda process   D. absorbal process

    8._____

9. How many poles does a 60 frequency, 1200 RPM motor have?

   A. 4   B. 6   C. 8   D. 10

10. A 3 phase, 4 wire distribution panel, having a line to line voltage of 208 volts, has a line to neutral of MOST NEARLY _____ volts.

    A. 208   B. 150   C. 120   D. 24

11. After a boiler is inspected, a notice is given to the owner. This should be posted

    A. on the door
    B. in the bathroom
    C. near the boiler
    D. in the owner's apartment or house

12. The MINIMUM diameter of a boiler safety is _____ inch.

    A. 3/4   B. 1/2   C. 1   D. 1 1/4

13. The MAXIMUM diameter of a boiler safety is _____ inches.

    A. 44   B. 4   C. 3 1/2   D. 3

14. On stoker fired boilers with gas ignition, the MAXIMUM flow of gas per minute is

    A. 1000   B. 1500   C. 200   D. 1500

15. On gas boilers producing over 400,000 BTU's per hour, the gas will be terminated if there is no flame detected for a period of _____ seconds.

    A. 2   B. 3   C. 4   D. 10

16. What is the MINIMUM thickness on steel plated boilers? _____ inch.

    A. 1/4   B. 1/2   C. 5/8   D. 7/8

17. What is the MINIMUM thickness on cast iron boilers? _____ inch.

    A. 1/4   B. 1/2   C. 5/8   D. 7/8

18. On a safety valve, there is a device that will lift the valve off the seat (without pressure) a MINIMUM of _____ inch.

    A. 1/16   B. 1/8   C. 1/4   D. 1/2

19. If a boiler in a battery can be disconnected, what kind of valve must be on the condensate return line?

    A. Angle   B. Globe   C. Gate   D. Check

20. The siphon on a steam gauge shall have a MINIMUM diameter of _____ inch.

    A. 1/4   B. 3/8   C. 1/2   D. 3/4

21. Hot water boilers in multiple dwellings do NOT have to be inspected if there are fewer than _____ families.

    A. 2   B. 6   C. 8   D. 10

22. The pressure gauge on a boiler shall show steam pressure

    A. 15% over steam pressure
    B. 1 1/2 times over steam pressure
    C. 2 times over steam pressure
    D. not less than 30 psig

23. The boiler will automatically shut down if the steam pressure is _____ percent over the maximum.

    A. 1   B. 2   C. 3   D. 5

24. On a gas boiler, how long does the pre-ignition period last before lighting off? _____ seconds.

    A. 30   B. 60   C. 90   D. 120

25. In an oil fired boiler using 3 gallons of oil an hour, how much time will lapse when there is no fire before the fuel supply stops? _____ seconds.

    A. 60   B. 120   C. 90   D. 30

KEY (CORRECT ANSWERS)

1. C		11. C	
2. C		12. A	
3. A		13. A	
4. A		14. A	
5. D		15. C	
6. A		16. A	
7. B		17. C	
8. B		18. A	
9. B		19. C	
10. C		20. A	

21. B
22. D
23. D
24. A
25. C

READING COMPREHENSION
UNDERSTANDING AND INTERPRETING WRITTEN MATERIAL
EXAMINATION SECTION
TEST 1

DIRECTIONS: Each question or incomplete statement is followed by several suggested answers or completions. Select the one that BEST answers the question or completes the statement. *PRINT THE LETTER OF THE CORRECT ANSWER IN THE SPACE AT THE RIGHT.*

Questions 1-2.

DIRECTIONS: Questions 1 and 2 are to be answered SOLELY on the basis of the following paragraph.

When fixing an upper sash cord, you must also remove the lower sash. To do this, the parting strip between the sash must be removed. Now remove the cover from the weight box channel, cut off the cord as before, and pull it over the pulleys. Pull your new cord over the pulleys and down into the channel where it may be fastened to the weight. The cord for an upper sash is cut off 1" or 2" below the pulley with the weight resting on the floor of the pocket and the cord held taut. These measurements allow for slight stretching of the cord. When the cord is cut to length, it can be pulled up over the pulley and tied with a single common knot in the end to fit into the socket in the sash groove. If the knot protrudes beyond the face of the sash, tap it gently to flatten. In this way, it will not become frayed from constant rubbing against the groove.

1. When repairing the upper sash cord, the FIRST thing to do is to
   A. remove the lower sash
   B. cut the existing sash cord
   C. remove the parting strip
   D. measure the length of new cord necessary

1._____

2. According to the above paragraph, the rope may become frayed if the
   A. pulley is too small   B. knot sticks out
   C. cord is too long   D. weight is too heavy

2._____

Questions 3-4.

DIRECTIONS: Questions 3 and 4 are to be answered SOLELY on the basis of the following paragraph.

Repeated burning of the same area should be avoided. Burning should not be done on impervious, shallow, unstable, or highly erodible soils, or on steep slopes—especially in areas subject to heavy rains or rapid snowmelt. When existing vegetation is likely to be killed or seriously weakened by the fire, measures should be taken to assure prompt revegetation of the burned area. Burns should be limited to relatively small proportions of a watershed unit so that the stream channels will be able to carry any increased flows with a minimum of damage.

3. According to the above paragraph, planned burning should be limited to small areas of the watershed because
    A. the fire can be better controlled
    B. existing vegetation will be less likely to be killed
    C. plants will grow quicker in small areas
    D. there will be less likelihood of damaging floods

3._____

4. According to the above paragraph, burning USUALLY should be done on soils that
    A. readily absorb moisture
    B. have been burnt before
    C. exist as a thin layer over rock
    D. can be flooded by nearby streams

4._____

Questions 5-11.

DIRECTIONS: Questions 5 through 11 are to be answered SOLELY on the basis of the following paragraph.

FUSE INFORMATION

Badly bent or distorted fuse clips cannot be permitted. Sometimes, the distortion or bending is so slight that it escapes notice, yet it may be the cause for fuse failures through the heat that is developed by the poor contact. Occasionally, the proper spring tension of the fuse clips has been destroyed by overheating from loose wire connections to the clips. Proper contact surfaces must be maintained to avoid faulty operation of the fuse. Maintenance men should remove oxides that form on the copper and brass contacts, check the clip pressure, and make sure that contact surfaces are not deformed or bent in any way. When removing oxides, use a well-worn file and remove only the oxide film. Do not use sandpaper or emery cloth as hard particles may come off and become embedded in the contact surfaces. All wire connections to the fuse holders should be carefully inspected to see that they are tight.

5. Fuse failure because of poor clip contact or loose connections is due to the resulting
    A. excessive voltage   B. increased current
    C. lowered resistance   D. heating effect

5._____

6. Oxides should be removed from fuse contacts by using
    A. a dull file   B. emery cloth
    C. fine sandpaper   D. a sharp file

6._____

7. One result of loose wire connections at the terminal of a fuse clip is stated in the above paragraph to be
    A. loss of tension in the wire
    B. welding of the fuse to the clip
    C. distortion of the clip
    D. loss of tension of the clip

7._____

8. Simple reasoning will show that the oxide film referred to is undesirable CHIEFLY because it
   A. looks dull
   B. makes removal of the fuse difficult
   C. weakens the clips
   D. introduces undesirable resistance

   8._____

9. Fuse clips that are bent very slightly
   A. should be replaced with new clips
   B. should be carefully filed
   C. may result in blowing of the fuse
   D. may prevent the fuse from blowing

   9._____

10. From the fuse information paragraph, it would be reasonable to conclude that fuse clips
    A. are difficult to maintain
    B. must be given proper maintenance
    C. require more attention than other electrical equipment
    D. are unreliable

    10._____

11. A safe practical way of checking the tightness of the wire connection to the fuse clips of a live 120-volt lighting circuit is to
    A. feel the connection with your hand to see if it is warm
    B. try tightening with an insulated screwdriver or socket wrench
    C. see if the circuit works
    D. measure the resistance with an ohmmeter

    11._____

Questions 12-13.

DIRECTIONS: Questions 12 through 13 are to be answered SOLELY on the basis of the following paragraph.

For cast iron pipe lines, the middle ring or sleeve shall have *beveled* ends and shall be high quality cast iron. The middle ring shall have a minimum wall thickness of 3/8" for pipe up to 8", 7/16" for pipe 10" to 30", and 1/2" for pipe over 30", nominal diameter. Minimum length of middle ring shall be 5" for pipe up to 10", 6" for pipe 10" to 30", and 10" for pipe 30" nominal diameter and larger. The middle ring shall not have a center pipe stop, unless otherwise specified.

12. As used in the above paragraph, the word *beveled* means MOST NEARLY
    A. straight   B. slanted   C. curved   D. rounded

    12._____

13. In accordance with the above paragraph, the middle ring of a 24" nominal diameter pipe would have a minimum wall thickness and length of _____ thick and _____ long.
    A. 3/8"; 5:
    B. 3/8"; 6"
    C. 7/16"; 6"
    D. 1/2"; 6"

    13._____

Questions 14-17.

DIRECTIONS: Questions 14 through 17 are to be answered SOLELY on the basis of the following paragraph.

Operators spotting loads with long booms and working around men need the smooth, easy operation and positive control of uniform pressure swing clutches. There are no jerks or grabs with these large disc-type clutches because there is always even pressure over the entire clutch lining surface. In the conventional band-type swing clutch, the pressure varies between dead and live ends of the band. The uniform pressure swing clutch has excellent provision for heat dissipation. The driving elements, which are always rotating, have a great number of fins cast in them. This gives them an impeller or blower action for cooling, resulting in longer life and freedom from frequent adjustment.

14. According to the above paragraph, it may be said that conventional band-type swing clutches have
    A. even pressure on the clutch lining
    B. larger contact area
    C. smaller contact area
    D. uneven pressure on the clutch lining

14.____

15. According to the above paragraph, machines equipped with uniform pressure swing clutches will
    A. give better service under all conditions
    B. require no clutch adjustment
    C. give positive control of hoist
    D. provide better control of swing

15.____

16. According to the above paragraph, it may be said that the rotation of the driving elements of the uniform pressure swing clutch is ALWAYS
    A. continuous   B. constant
    C. varying   D. uncertain

16.____

17. According to the above paragraph, freedom from frequent adjustment is due to the
    A. operator's smooth, easy operation
    B. positive control of the clutch
    C. cooling effect of the rotating fins
    D. larger contact area of the bigger clutch

17.____

Questions 18-22.

DIRECTIONS: Questions 18 through 22 are to be answered SOLELY on the basis of the following paragraphs.

Exhaust valve clearance adjustment on diesel engines is very important for proper operation of the engine. Insufficient clearance between the exhaust valve stem and the rocker arm causes a loss of compression and, after a while, burning of the valves and valve seat inserts. On the other hand, too much valve clearance will result in noisy operation of the engine.

Exhaust valves that are maintained in good operating condition will result in efficient combustion in the engine. Valve seats must be true and unpitted, and valve stems must work smoothly within the valve guides. Long valve life will result from proper maintenance and operation of the engine.

Engine operating temperatures should be maintained between 160°F and 185°F. Low operating temperatures result in incomplete combustion and the deposit of fuel lacquers on valves.

18. According to the above paragraphs, too much valve clearance will cause the engine to operate
   A. slowly   B. noisily   C. smoothly   D. cold

19. On the basis of the information given in the above paragraphs, operating temperatures of a diesel engine should be between
   A. 125°F and 130°F   B. 140°F and 150°F
   C. 160°F and 185°F   D. 190°F and 205°F

20. According to the above paragraphs, the deposit of fuel lacquers on valves is caused by
   A. high operating temperatures
   B. insufficient valve clearance
   C. low operating temperatures
   D. efficient combustion

21. According to the above paragraphs, for efficient operation of the engine, valve seats must
   A. have sufficient clearance
   B. be true and unpitted
   C. operate at low temperatures
   D. be adjusted regularly

22. According to the above paragraphs, a loss of compression is due to insufficient clearance between the exhaust valve stem and the
   A. rocker arm   B. valve seat
   C. valve seat inserts D. valve guides

Questions 23-25.

DIRECTIONS: Questions 23 through 25 are to be answered SOLELY on the basis of the following excerpt:

A SPECIFICATION FOR ELECTRIC WORK FOR THE CITY

Breakers shall be equipped with magnetic blowout coils...Handles of breakers shall be trip-free...Breakers shall be designed to carry 100% of trip rating continuously; to have inverse time delay tripping above 100% of trip rating...

23. According to the above paragraph, the breaker shall have provision for
   A. resetting   B. arc quenching
   C. adjusting trip time D. adjusting trip rating

24. According to the above paragraph, the breaker
   A. shall trip easily at exactly 100% of trip rating
   B. shall trip instantly at a little more than 100% of trip rating
   C. should be constructed so that it shall not be possible to prevent it from opening on overload or short circuit by holding the handle in the ON position
   D. shall not trip prematurely at 100% of trip rating

25. According to the above paragraph, the breaker shall trip 25._____
    A. instantaneously as soon as 100% of trip rating is reached
    B. instantaneously as soon as 100% of trip rating is exceeded
    C. more quickly the greater the current, once 100% of trip rating is exceeded
    D. after a predetermined fixed time lapse, once 100% of trip rating is reached

---

KEY (CORRECT ANSWERS)

1.	C	11.	B
2.	B	12.	B
3.	D	13.	C
4.	A	14.	D
5.	D	15.	D
6.	A	16.	A
7.	D	17.	C
8.	D	18.	B
9.	C	19.	C
10.	B	20.	C

21. B
22. A
23. B
24. C
25. C

TEST 2

DIRECTIONS: Each question or incomplete statement is followed by several suggested answers or completions. Select the one that BEST answers the question or completes the statement. *PRINT THE LETTER OF THE CORRECT ANSWER IN THE SPACE AT THE RIGHT.*

Questions 1-4.

DIRECTIONS: Questions 1 through 4 are to be answered SOLELY on the basis of the following paragraph.

    A low pressure hot water boiler shall include a relief valve or valves of a capacity such that with the heat generating equipment operating at maximum, the pressure cannot rise more than 20 percent above the maximum allowable working pressure (set pressure) if that is 30 p.s.i. gage or less, nor more than 10 percent if it is more than 30 p.s.i. gage. The difference between the set pressure and the pressure at which the valve is relieving is known as *over-pressure or accumulation*. If the steam relieving capacity in pounds per hour is calculated, it shall be determined by dividing by 1,000 the maximum BTU output at the boiler nozzle obtainable from the heat generating equipment, or by multiplying the square feet of heating surface by five.

1. In accordance with the above paragraph, the capacity of a relief valve should be computed on the basis of
   - A. size of boiler
   - B. maximum rated capacity of generating equipment
   - C. average output of the generating equipment
   - D. minimum capacity of generating equipment

1._____

2. In accordance with the above paragraph, with a set pressure of 30 p.s.i. gage, the overpressure should not be more than _____ p.s.i.
   - A. 3   B. 6   C. 33   D. 36

2._____

3. In accordance with the above paragraph, a relief valve should start relieving at a pressure equal to the
   - A. set pressure
   - B. over pressure
   - C. over pressure minus set pressure
   - D. set pressure plus over pressure

3._____

4. In accordance with the above paragraph, the steam relieving capacity can be computed by
   - A. *multiplying* the maximum BTU output by 5
   - B. *dividing* the pounds of steam per hour by 1,000
   - C. *dividing* the maximum BTU output by the square feet of heating surface
   - D. *dividing* the maximum BTU output by 1,000

4._____

Questions 5-8.

DIRECTIONS: Questions 5 through 8 are to be answered SOLELY on the basis of the following paragraph.

Air conditioning units requiring a minimum rate of flow of water in excess of one-half (1/2) gallon per minute shall be metered. Air conditioning equipment with a refrigeration unit which has a definite rate of capacity in tons or fractions thereof, the charge will be at the rate of $30 per annum per ton capacity from the date installed to the date when the supply is metered. Such units, when equipped with an approved water-conserving device, shall be charged at the rate of $4.50 per annum per ton capacity from the date installed to the date when the supply is metered.

5. A man who was in the market for air conditioning equipment was considering three different units. Unit 1 required a flow of 28 gallons of water per hour; Unit 2 required 30 gallons of water per hour; Unit 3 required 32 gallons of water per hour. The man asked the salesman which units would require the installation of a water meter. According to the above passage, the salesman SHOULD answer:
   A. All three units require meters
   B. Units 2 and 3 require meters
   C. Unit 3 only requires a meter
   D. None of the units require a meter

6. Suppose that air conditioning equipment with a refrigeration unit of 10 tons was put in operation on October 1; and in the following year on July 1, a meter was installed. According to the above passage, the charge for this period would be _____ the annual rate.
   A. twice   B. equal to
   C. three-fourths   D. one-fourth

7. The charge for air conditioning equipment which has no refrigeration unit
   A. is $30 per year
   B. is $25.50 per year
   C. is $4.50 per year
   D. cannot be determined from the above passage

8. The charge for air conditioning equipment with a seven-ton refrigeration unit equipped with an approved water-conserving device
   A. is $4.50 per year
   B. is $25.50 per year
   C. is $31.50 per year
   D. cannot be determined from the above passage

Questions 9-14.

DIRECTIONS: Questions 9 through 14 are to be answered SOLELY on the basis of the following paragraph.

The city makes unremitting efforts to keep the water free from pollution. An inspectional force under a sanitary expert is engaged in patrolling the watersheds to see that the department's sanitary regulations are observed. Samples taken daily from various points in the water supply system are examined and analyzed at the three laboratories maintained by the department. All water before delivery to the distribution mains is treated with chlorine to destroy bacteria. In addition, some water is aerated to free it from gases and, in some cases, from microscopic organisms. Generally, microscopic organisms which develop in the reservoirs and at times impart an unpleasant taste and odor to the water, though in no sense harmful to health, are destroyed by treatment with copper sulfate and by chlorine dosage. None of the supplies is filtered, but the quality of the water supplied by the city is excellent for all purposes, and it is clear and wholesome.

9. According to the above paragraph, microscopic organisms are removed from the water supplied to the city by means of
   A. chlorine alone
   B. chlorine, aeration, and filtration
   C. chlorine, aeration, filtration, and sampling
   D. copper sulfate, chlorine, and aeration

10. Microscopic organisms in the water supply GENERALLY are
    A. a health menace
    B. impossible to detect
    C. not harmful to health
    D. not destroyed in the water

11. The MAIN function of the inspectional force, as described in the above paragraph, is to
    A. take samples of water for analysis
    B. enforce sanitary regulations
    C. add chlorine to the water supply
    D. inspect water-use meters

12. According to the above paragraph, chlorine is added to water before entering the
    A. watersheds
    B. reservoirs
    C. distribution mains
    D. run-off areas

13. Of the following suggested headings or titles for the above paragraph, the one that BEST tells what the paragraph is about is
    A. QUALITY OF WATER
    B. CHLORINATION OF WATER
    C. TESTING OF WATER
    D. BACTERIA IN WATER

14. The MOST likely reason for taking samples of water for examination and analysis from various points in the water supply system is:
    A. The testing points are convenient to the department's laboratories
    B. Water from one part of the system may be made undrinkable by a local condition
    C. The samples can be distributed equally among the three laboratories
    D. The hardness or softness of water varies from place to place

Questions 15-17.

DIRECTIONS: Questions 15 through 17 are to be answered SOLELY on the basis of the following paragraph.

A building measuring 200' x 100' at the street is set back 20' on all sides at the 15th floor, and an additional 10' on all sides at the 30th floor. The building is 35 stories high.

15. The floor area of the 16th floor is MOST NEARLY _____ sq. ft. 15._____
    A. 20,000   B. 14,400   C. 9,600   D. 7,500

16. The floor area of the 35th floor is MOST NEARLY _____ sq. ft. 16._____
    A. 20,000   B. 13,900   C. 7,500   D. 5,600

17. The floor area of the 16th floor, compared to the floor area of the 2nd floor, is MOST NEARLY _____ as much. 17._____
    A. three-fourths (3/4)   B. two-thirds (2/3)
    C. one-half (1/2)   D. four-tenths (4/10)

Question 18.

DIRECTIONS: Question 18 is to be answered SOLELY on the basis of the following paragraph.

Experience has shown that, in general, a result of the installation of meters on services not previously metered is to reduce the amount of water consumed, but is not necessarily to reduce the peak load on plumbing systems. The permissible head loss through meters at their rated maximum flow is 20 p.s.i. The installation of a meter may therefore appreciably lower the pressures available in fixtures on a plumbing system.

18. According to the above paragraph, a water meter may 18._____
    A. limit the flow in the plumbing system of 20 p.s.i.
    B. reduce the peak load on the plumbing system
    C. increase the overall amount of water consumed
    D. reduce the pressure in the plumbing system

Question 19.

DIRECTIONS: Question 19 is to be answered SOLELY on the basis of the following paragraph.

Spring comes without trumpets to a city. The asphalt is a wilderness that does not quicken overnight; winds blow gritty with cinders instead of merry with the smells of earth and fertilizer. Women wear their gardens on their hats. But spring is a season in the city, and it has its own harbingers, constant as daffodils. Shop windows change their colors, people walk more slowly on the streets, what one can see of the sky has a bluer tone. Pulitzer prizes awake and sing and matinee tickets go-a-begging. But gayer than any of these are the carousels, which are already in sheltered places, beginning to turn with the sound of springtime itself. They are the earliest and the truest and the oldest of all the urban signs.

19. In the passage above, the word *harbingers* means 19._____
    A. storms   B. truths   C. virtues   D. forerunners

Questions 20-22.

DIRECTIONS: Questions 20 through 22 are to be answered SOLELY on the basis of the following paragraph.

Gas heaters include manually operated, automatic, and instantaneous heaters. Some heaters are equipped with a thermostat which controls the fuel supply so that when the water falls below a predetermined temperature, the fuel is automatically turned on. In some types, the hot-water storage tank is well-insulated to economize the use of fuel. Instantaneous heaters are arranged so that the opening of a faucet on the hot-water pipe will increase the flow of fuel, which is ignited by a continuously burning pilot light to heat the water to from 120° to 130°F. The possibility that the pilot light will die out offers a source of danger in the use of automatic appliances which depend on a pilot light. Gas and oil heaters are dangerous, and they should be designed to prevent the accumulation, in a confined space within the heater, of a large volume of an explosive mixture.

20. According to the above passage, the opening of a hot-water faucet on a hot-water pipe connected to an instantaneous hot-water heater will the pilot light.
    A. *increase* the temperature of
    B. *increase* the flow of fuel to
    C. *decrease* the flow of fuel to
    D. *have a marked effect* on

21. According to the above passage, the fuel is automatically turned on in a heater equipped with a thermostat whenever
    A. the water temperature drops below 120°F
    B. the pilot light is lit
    C. the water temperature drops below some predetermined temperature
    D. a hot water supply is opened

22. According to the above passage, some hot-water storage tanks are well-insulated to
    A. accelerate the burning of the fuel
    B. maintain the water temperature between 120° and 130°F
    C. prevent the pilot light from being extinguished
    D. minimize the expenditure of fuel

Question 23.

DIRECTIONS: Question 23 is to be answered SOLELY on the basis of the following paragraph.

Breakage of the piston under high-speed operation has been the commonest fault of disc piston meters. Various techniques are adopted to prevent this, such as *throttling* the meter, cutting away the edge of the piston, or reinforcing it, but these are simply makeshifts.

23. As used in the above paragraph, the word *throttling* means MOST NEARLY
    A. enlarging   B. choking
    C. harnessing   D. dismantling

Questions 24-25.

DIRECTIONS: Questions 24 and 25 are to be answered SOLELY on the basis of the following paragraph.

One of the most common and objectionable difficulties occurring in a drainage system is trap seal loss. This failure can be attributed directly to inadequate ventilation of the trap and the subsequent negative and positive pressures which occur. A trap seal may be lost either by siphonage and/or back pressure. Loss of the trap seal by siphonage is the result of a negative pressure in the drainage system. The seal content of the trap is forced by siphonage into the waste piping of the drainage system through exertion of atmospheric pressure on the fixture side of the trap seal.

24. According to the above paragraph, a positive pressure is a direct result of
    A. siphonage
    B. unbalanced trap seal
    C. poor ventilation
    D. atmospheric pressure

25. According to the above paragraph, the water in the trap is forced into the drain pipe by
    A. atmospheric pressure
    B. back pressure
    C. negative pressure
    D. back pressure on fixture side of seal

KEY (CORRECT ANSWERS)

1. B
2. B
3. D
4. D
5. C

6. C
7. D
8. C
9. D
10. C

11. B
12. C
13. A
14. B
15. C

16. D
17. C
18. D
19. B
20. B

21. C
22. D
23. B
24. C
25. A

EXAMINATION SECTION
TEST 1

DIRECTIONS: Each question or incomplete statement is followed by several suggested answers or completions. Select the one that BEST answers the question or completes the statement. *PRINT THE LETTER OF THE CORRECT ANSWER IN THE SPACE AT THE RIGHT.*

1. Which of the following sentences is punctuated INCORRECTLY? 1.____
   A. Johnson said, "One tiny virus, Blanche, can multiply so fast that it will become 200 viruses in 25 minutes."
   B. With economic pressures hitting them from all sides, American farmers have become the weak link in the food chain.
   C. The degree to which this is true, of course, depends on the personalities of the people involved, the subject matter, and the atmosphere in general.
   D. "What loneliness, asked George Eliot, is more lonely than distrust?"

2. Which of the following sentences is punctuated INCORRECTLY? 2.____
   A. Based on past experiences, do you expect the plumber to show up late, not have the right parts, and overcharge you.
   B. When polled, however, the participants were most concerned that it be convenient.
   C. No one mentioned the flavor of the coffee, and no one seemed to care that china was used instead of plastic.
   D. As we said before, sometimes people view others as things; they don't see them as living, breathing beings like themselves.

3. Convention members travelled here from Kingston New York Pittsfield Massachusetts Bennington Vermont and Hartford Connecticut. 3.____
   How many commas should there be in the above sentence?
   A. 3   B. 4   C. 5   D. 6

4. Of the two speakers the one who spoke about human rights is more famous and more humble. 4.____
   How many commas should there be in the above sentence?
   A. 1   B. 2   C. 3   D. 4

5. Which sentence is punctuated INCORRECTLY? 5.____
   A. Five people voted no; two voted yes; one person abstained.
   B. Well, consider what has been said here today, but we won't make any promises.
   C. Anthropologists divide history into three major periods: the Stone Age, the Bronze Age, and the Iron Age.
   D. Therefore, we may create a stereotype about people who are unsuccessful; we may see them as lazy, unintelligent, or afraid of success.

6. Which sentence is punctuated INCORRECTLY? 6._____
   A. Studies have found that the unpredictability of customer behavior can lead to a great deal of stress, particularly if the behavior is unpleasant or if the employee has little control over it.
   B. If this degree of emotion and variation can occur in spectator sports, imagine the role that perceptions can play when there are <u>real</u> stakes involved.
   C. At other times, however hidden expectations may sabotage or severely damage an encounter without anyone knowing what happened.
   D. There are usually four issues to look for in a conflict: differences in values, goals, methods, and facts.

Questions 7-10.

DIRECTIONS: Questions 7 through 10 test your ability to distinguish between words that sound alike but are spelled differently and have different meanings. In the following groups of sentences, one of the underlined words is used incorrectly.

7. A. By <u>accepting</u> responsibility for their actions, managers promote trust. 7._____
   B. Dropping hints or making <u>illusions</u> to things that you would like changed sometimes leads to resentment.
   C. The entire unit <u>loses</u> respect for the manager and resents the reprimand.
   D. Many people are <u>averse</u> to confronting problems directly; they would rather avoid them.

8. A. What does this say about the <u>effect</u> our expectations have on those we supervise? 8._____
   B. In an effort to save time between 9 A.M. and 1 P.M., the staff members devised <u>their</u> own interpretation of what was to be done on these forms.
   C. The taskmaster's <u>principal</u> concern is for getting the work done; he or she is not concerned about the need or interests of employees.
   D. The advisor's main objective was increasing Angela's ability to invest her <u>capitol</u> wisely.

9. A. A typical problem is that people have to cope with the internal <u>censer</u> of their feelings. 9._____
   B. Sometimes, in their attempt to sound more learned, people speak in ways that are barely <u>comprehensible</u>.
   C. The <u>council</u> will meet next Friday to decide whether Abrams should continue as representative.
   D. His <u>descent</u> from grace was assured by that final word.

10. A. The doctor said that John's leg had to remain <u>stationary</u> or it would not heal properly. 10._____
    B. There is a city <u>ordinance</u> against parking too close to fire hydrants.
    C. Meyer's problem is that he is never <u>discrete</u> when talking about office politics.
    D. Mrs. Thatcher probably worked harder <u>than</u> any other British Prime Minister had ever worked.

3 (#1)

Questions 11-20.

DIRECTIONS: For each of the following groups of sentences in Questions 11 through 20, select the sentence which is the BEST example of English usage and grammar.

11. A. She is a woman who, at age sixty, is distinctly attractive and cares about how they look.
    B. It was a seemingly impossible search, and no one knew the problems better than she.
    C. On the surface, they are all sweetness and light, but his morbid character is under it.
    D. The minicopier, designed to appeal to those who do business on the run like architects in the field or business travelers, weigh about four pounds.

11.____

12. A. Neither the administrators nor the union representative regret the decision to settle the disagreement.
    B. The plans which are made earlier this year were no longer being considered.
    C. I would have rode with him if I had known he was leaving at five.
    D. I don't know who she said had it.

12.____

13. A. Writing at a desk, the memo was handed to her for immediate attention.
    B. Carla didn't water Carl's plants this week, which she never does.
    C. Not only are they good workers, with excellent writing and speaking skills, and they get to the crux of any problem we hand them.
    D. We've noticed that this enthusiasm for undertaking new projects sometimes interferes with his attention to detail.

13.____

14. A. It's obvious that Nick offends people by being unruly, inattentive, and having no patience.
    B. Marcia told Genie that she would have to leave soon.
    C. Here are the papers you need to complete your investigation.
    D. Julio was startled by you're comment.

14.____

15. A. The new manager has done good since receiving her promotion, but her secretary has helped her a great deal.
    B. One of the personnel managers approached John and tells him that the client arrived unexpectedly.
    C. If somebody can supply us with the correct figures, they should do so immediately.
    D. Like zealots, advocates seek power because they want to influence the policies and actions of an organization.

15.____

16. A. Between you and me, Chris probably won't finish this assignment in time.   16.___
    B. Rounding the corner, the snack bar appeared before us.
    C. Parker's radical reputation made to the Supreme Court his appointment impossible.
    D. By the time we arrived, Marion finishes briefing James and returns to Hank's office.

17. A. As we pointed out earlier, the critical determinant of the success of middle   17.___
       managers is their ability to communicate well with others.
    B. The lecturer stated there wasn't no reason for bad supervision.
    C. We are well aware whose at fault in this instance.
    D. When planning important changes, it's often wise to seek the participation of others because employees often have much valuable ideas to offer.

18. A. Joan had ought to throw out those old things that were damaged when the   18.___
       roof leaked.
    B. I spose he'll let us know what he's decided when he finally comes to a decision.
    C. Carmen was walking to work when she suddenly realized that she had left her lunch on the table as she passed the market.
    D. Are these enough plants for your new office?

19. A. First move the lever forward, and then they should lift the ribbon casing   19.___
       before trying to take it out.
    B. Michael finished quickest than any other person in the office.
    C. There is a special meeting for we committee members today at 4 p.m.
    D. My husband is worried about our having to work overtime next week.

20. A. Another source of conflicts are individuals who possess very poor   20.___
       interpersonal skills.
    B. It is difficult for us to work with him on projects because these kinds of people are not interested in team building.
    C. Each of the departments was represented at the meeting.
    D. Poor boy, he never should of past that truck on the right.

Questions 21-28.

DIRECTIONS: In Questions 21 through 28, there may be a problem with English grammar or usage. If a problem does exist, select the letter that indicates the most effective change. If no problem exists, select Choice A.

21. He rushed her to the hospital and stayed with her, even though this took quite a   21.___
    bit of his time, he didn't charge her anything.
    A. No changes are necessary.
    B. Change even though to although
    C. Change the first comma to a period and capitalize even
    D. Change rushed to had rushed

22. Waiting that appears unfairly feels longer than waiting that seems justified.
    A. No changes are necessary.
    B. Change unfairly to unfair
    C. Change appears to seems
    D. Change longer to longest

23. May be you and the person who argued with you will be able to reach an agreement.
    A. No changes are necessary
    B. Change will be to were
    C. Change argued with to had an argument with
    D. Change May be to Maybe

24. Any one of them could of taken the file while you were having coffee.
    A. No changes are necessary
    B. Change any one to anyone
    C. Change of to have
    D. Change were having to were out having

25. While people get jobs or move from poverty level to better paying employment, they stop receiving benefits and start paying taxes.
    A. No changes are necessary
    B. Change While to As
    C. Change stop to will stop
    D. Change get to obtain

26. Maribeth's phone rang while talking to George about the possibility of their meeting Tom at three this afternoon.
    A. No changes are necessary
    B. Change their to her
    C. Move to George so that it follows Tom
    D. Change talking to she was talking

27. According to their father, Lisa is smarter than Chris, but Emily is the smartest of the three sisters.
    A. No changes are necessary
    B. Change their to her
    C. Change is to was
    D. Make two sentences, changing the second comma to a period and omitting but

28. Yesterday, Mark and he claim that Carl took Carol's ideas and used them inappropriately.
    A. No changes are necessary
    B. Change claim to claimed
    C. Change inappropriately to inappropriate
    D. Change Carol's to Carols'

Questions 29-34.

DIRECTIONS: For each group of sentences in Questions 29 through 34, select the choice that represents the BEST editing of the problem sentence.

29. The managers expected employees to be at their desks at all times, but they would always be late or leave unannounced.
    A. The managers wanted employees to always be at their desks, but they would always be late or leave unannounced.
    B. Although the managers expected employees to be at their desks no matter what came up, they would always be late and leave without telling anyone.
    C. Although the managers expected employees to be at their desks at all times, the managers would always be late or leave without telling anyone.
    D. The managers expected the employee to never leave their desks, but they would always be late or leave without telling anyone.

29.____

30. The one who is department manager he will call you to discuss the problem tomorrow morning at 10 A.M.
    A. The one who is department manager will call you tomorrow morning at ten to discuss the problem.
    B. The department manager will call you to discuss the problem tomorrow at 10 A.M.
    C. Tomorrow morning at 10 A.M., the department manager will call you to discuss the problem.
    D. Tomorrow morning the department manager will call you to discuss the problem.

30.____

31. A conference on child care in the workplace the $200 cost of which to attend may be prohibitive to childcare workers who earn less than that weekly.
    A. A conference on child care in the workplace that costs $200 may be too expensive for childcare workers who earn less than that each week.
    B. A conference on child care in the workplace, the cost of which to attend is $200, may be prohibitive to childcare workers who earn less than that weekly.
    C. A conference on child care in the workplace who costs $200 may be too expensive for childcare workers who earn less than that a week.
    D. A conference on child care in the workplace which costs $200 may be too expensive to childcare workers who earn less than that on a weekly basis.

31.____

32. In accordance with estimates recently made, there are 40,000 to 50,000 nuclear weapons in our world today.
    A. Because of estimates recently, there are 40,000 to 50,000 nuclear weapons in the world today.
    B. In accordance with estimates made recently, there are 40,000 to 50,000 nuclear weapons in the world today.

32.____

C. According to estimates made recently, there are 40,000 to 50,000 weapons in the world today.
D. According to recent estimates, there are 40,000 to 50,000 nuclear weapons in the world today.

33. Motivation is important in problem solving, but they say that excessive motivation can inhibit the creative process.
    A. Motivation is important in problem solving, but, as they say, too much of it can inhibit the creative process.
    B. Motivation is important in problem solving and excessive motivation will inhibit the creative process.
    C. Motivation is important in problem solving, but excessive motivation can inhibit the creative process.
    D. Motivation is important in problem solving because excessive motivation can inhibit the creative process.

33.____

34. In selecting the best option calls for consulting with all the people that are involved in it.
    A. In selecting the best option consulting with all people concerned with it.
    B. Calling for the best option, we consulted all the affected people.
    C. We called all the people involved to select the best option.
    D. To be sure of selecting the best option, one should consult all the people involved.

34.____

35. There are a number of problems with the following letter. From the options below, select the version that is MOST in accordance with standard business style, tone, and form.

35.____

Dear Sir:

   We are so sorry that we have had to backorder your order for 15,000 widgets and 2,300 whatzits for such a long time. We have been having incredibly bad luck lately. When your order first came in no one could get to it because my secretary was out with the flu and her replacement didn't know what she was doing, then there was the dock strike in Cucamonga which held things up for awhile, and then it just somehow got lost. We think it may have fallen behind the radiator.
   We are happy to say that all these problems have been taken care of, we are caught up on supplies, and we should have the stuff to you soon, in the near future—about two weeks. You may not believe us after everything you've been through with us, but it's true.
   We'll let you know as soon as we have a secure date for delivery. Thank you so much for continuing to do business with us after all the problems this probably has caused you.

Yours very sincerely,
Rob Barker

A. Dear Sir:

   We are so sorry that we have had to backorder your order for 15,000 widgets and 2,300 whatzits. We have been having problems with staff lately and the dock strike hasn't helped anything.
   We are happy to say that all these problems have been taken care of. I've told my secretary to get right on it, and we should have the stuff to you soon. Thank you so much for continuing to do business with us after all the problems this must have caused you.
   We'll let you know as soon as we have a secure date for delivery.

   Sincerely,
   Rob Barker

B. Dear Sir:

   We regret that we haven't been able to fill your order for 15,000 widgets and 2,300 whatzits in a timely fashion.
   We'll let you know as soon as we have a secure date for delivery.

   Sincerely,
   Rob Barker

C. Dear Sir:

   We are so very sorry that we haven't been able to fill your order for 15,000 widgets and 2,300 whatzits. We have been having incredibly bad luck lately, but things are much better now.
   Thank you so much for bearing with us through all of this. We'll let you know as soon as we have a secure date for delivery.

   Sincerely,
   Rob Barker

D. Dear Sir:

   We are very sorry that we haven't been able to fill your order for 15,000 widgets and 2,300 whatzits. Due to unforeseen difficulties, we have had to back-order your request. At this time, supplies have caught up to demand, and we foresee a delivery date within the next two weeks.
   We'll let you know as soon as we have a secure date for delivery. Thank you for your patience.

   Sincerely,
   Rob Barker

KEY (CORRECT ANSWERS)

1.	D	11.	B	21.	C	31.	A
2.	A	12.	D	22.	B	32.	D
3.	B	13.	D	23.	D	33.	C
4.	A	14.	C	24.	C	34.	D
5.	B	15.	D	25.	B	35.	D
6.	C	16.	A	26.	D		
7.	B	17.	A	27.	A		
8.	D	18.	D	28.	B		
9.	A	19.	D	29.	C		
10.	C	20.	C	30.	B		

ARITHMETICAL REASONING
EXAMINATION SECTION
TEST 1

DIRECTIONS: Each question or incomplete statement is followed by several suggested answers or completions. Select the one that BEST answers the question or completes the statement. *PRINT THE LETTER OF THE CORRECT ANSWER IN THE SPACE AT THE RIGHT.*

1.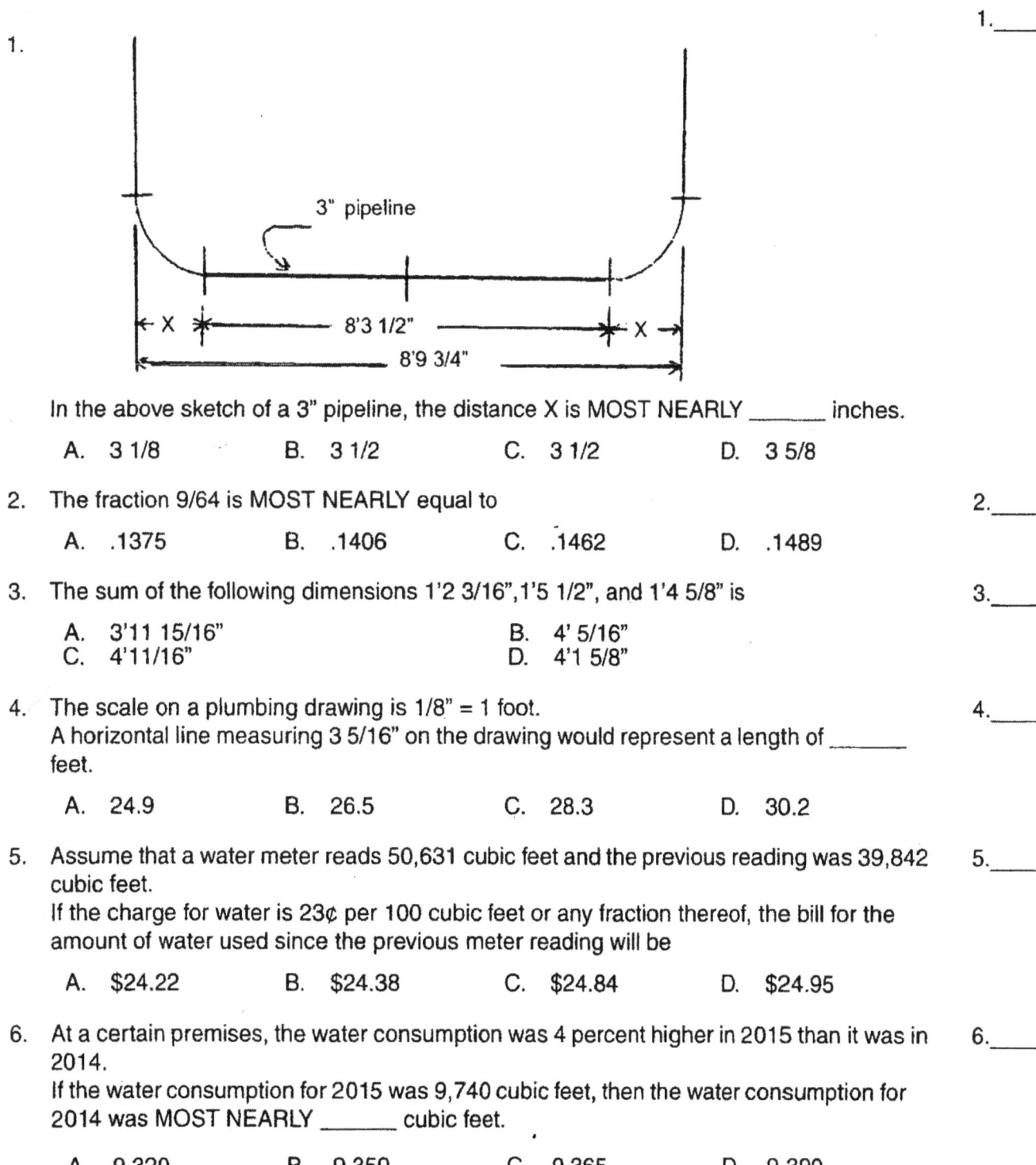

   In the above sketch of a 3" pipeline, the distance X is MOST NEARLY _____ inches.

   A. 3 1/8   B. 3 1/2   C. 3 1/2   D. 3 5/8

2. The fraction 9/64 is MOST NEARLY equal to

   A. .1375   B. .1406   C. .1462   D. .1489

3. The sum of the following dimensions 1'2 3/16", 1'5 1/2", and 1'4 5/8" is

   A. 3'11 15/16"   B. 4' 5/16"
   C. 4'11/16"   D. 4'1 5/8"

4. The scale on a plumbing drawing is 1/8" = 1 foot.
   A horizontal line measuring 3 5/16" on the drawing would represent a length of _____ feet.

   A. 24.9   B. 26.5   C. 28.3   D. 30.2

5. Assume that a water meter reads 50,631 cubic feet and the previous reading was 39,842 cubic feet.
   If the charge for water is 23¢ per 100 cubic feet or any fraction thereof, the bill for the amount of water used since the previous meter reading will be

   A. $24.22   B. $24.38   C. $24.84   D. $24.95

6. At a certain premises, the water consumption was 4 percent higher in 2015 than it was in 2014.
   If the water consumption for 2015 was 9,740 cubic feet, then the water consumption for 2014 was MOST NEARLY _____ cubic feet.

   A. 9,320   B. 9,350   C. 9,365   D. 9,390

7. A pump delivers water at a constant rate of 40 gallons per minute.
   If there are 7.5 gallons to a cubic foot of water, the time it will take to fill a tank 6 feet x 5 feet x 4 feet is MOST NEARLY _____ minutes.

   A. 15   B. 22.5   C. 28.5   D. 30

8. The total weight, in pounds, of three lengths of 3" cast-iron pipe 7'6" long, weighing 14.5 pounds per foot, and four lengths of 4" cast-iron pipe each 5'0" long, weighing 13.0 pounds per foot, is MOST NEARLY

   A. 540   B. 585   C. 600   D. 665

9. The water pressure at the bottom of a column of water 34 feet high is 14.7 lbs./sq.in. The water pressure in lbs./sq.in. at the bottom of the column of water 12 feet high is MOST NEARLY

   A. 3   B. 5   C. 7   D. 9

10. The number of cubic yards of earth that would be removed when digging a trench 8 feet wide x 9 feet deep x 63 feet long is

    A. 56   B. 168   C. 314   D. 504

11. On test, a meter registered one cubic foot for each 1 1/3 cubic feet of water that passed through it.
    If the meter had a reading of 1,200 cubic feet, we may conclude that the CORRECT amount should be _____ cubic feet.

    A. 800   B. 900   C. 1,500   D. 1,600

12. A water use meter reads 87,463 cubic feet.
    If the previous reading was 17,377 cubic feet and the rate charged is 15 cents per 100 cubic feet, the bill for water use during this period is about

    A. $45.00   B. $65.00   C. $85.00   D. $105.00

13. Under proper conditions, the one of the following groups of pipes that gives the same flow in gals/min as one 6" diameter pipe is (neglect friction) _____ pipes of _____ diameter each.

    A. 3; 3"   B. 4; 3"   C. 2; 4"   D. 3; 4"

14. A roof tank is used to furnish the domestic water supply to a ten story building. This tank has a capacity of 5,900 gallons. At 10:00 A.M. one morning, the tank is half full.
    If water is being used at the rate of 50 gals/min, the pump which is used to fill the tank has a rated capacity of 90 gals/min, the time it would take to fill the tank under these conditions is MOST NEARLY _____ hour(s), _____ minutes.

    A. 2; 8   B. 1; 14   C. 2; 32   D. 1; 2

15. The number of gallons of water contained in a cylindrical swimming pool 8 feet in diameter and filled to a depth of 3 feet 6 inches is MOST NEARLY (assume 7.5 gallons = 1 cubic foot)

    A. 30   B. 225   C. 1,320   D. 3,000

16. The charge for metered water is 52 1/2 cents per hundred cubic feet, with a minimum charge of $21 per annum. Of the following, the SMALLEST water usage in hundred cubic feet that would result in a charge GREATER than the minimum is   16.____

    A. 39 B. 40 C. 41 D. 42

17. The annual frontage rent on a one-story building 40 ft. in length is $735.00. For each additional story, $52.50 per annum is added to the frontage rent. For demolition, the charge for wetting down is 3/8 of the annual frontage charge.
    The charge for wetting down a building six stories in height, with a 40 ft. frontage, is MOST NEARLY   17.____

    A. $369 B. $371 C. $372 D. $374

18. If the drawing of a piping layout is made to a scale of 1/4" equals one foot, then a 7'9" length of piping would be represented by a scaled length on the drawing of APPROXIMATELY _____ inches.   18.____

    A. 2 B. 7 3/4 C. 23 1/4 D. 31

19. A plumbing sketch is drawn to a scale of eighth-size. A line measuring 3" on the sketch would be equivalent to _____ feet.   19.____

    A. 2 B. 6 C. 12 D. 24

20. If 500 feet of pipe weighs 800 lbs., the number of pounds that 120 feet will weigh is MOST NEARLY   20.____

    A. 190 B. 210 C. 230 D. 240

21. If a trench is excavated 3'0" wide by 5'6" deep and 50 feet long, the total number of cubic yards of earth removed is MOST NEARLY   21.____

    A. 30 B. 90 C. 150 D. 825

22. Assume that a plumber earns $86,500 per year.
    If eighteen percent of his pay is deducted for taxes and social security, his net weekly pay will be APPROXIMATELY   22.____

    A. $1,326 B. $1,365 C. $1,436 D. $1,457.50

23. Assume that a plumbing installation is made up of the following fixtures and groups of fixtures: 12 bathroom groups each containing one W.C., one lavatory, and one bathtub with shower; 12 bathroom groups each containing one W.C., one lavatory, one bathtub, and one shower stall; 24 combination kitchen fixtures; 4 floor drains; 6 slop sinks without flushing rim; and 2 shower stalls (or shower bath).
    The total number of fixtures for the above plumbing installation is MOST NEARLY   23.____

    A. 60 B. 95 C. 120 D. 210

24. A triangular opening in a wall forms a 30-60 degree right triangle.
    If the longest side measures 12'0", then the shortest side will measure   24.____

    A. 3'0" B. 4'0" C. 6'0" D. 8'0"

25. You are directed to cut 4 pieces of pipe, one each of the following length: 2'6 1/4", 3'9 3/8", 4'7 5/8", and 5'8 7/8".
The total length of these 4 pieces is

    A. 15'7 1/4"   B. 15'9 3/8"   C. 16'5 7/8"   D. 16'8 1/8"

KEY (CORRECT ANSWERS)

1. A
2. B
3. B
4. B
5. C
6. C
7. B
8. B
9. B
10. B
11. D
12. D
13. B
14. B
15. C
16. C
17. D
18. A
19. A
20. A
21. A
22. B
23. C
24. C
25. D

SOLUTIONS TO PROBLEMS

1. 8'3 1/2" + x + x = 8'9 3/4" Then, 2x = 6 1/4", so x = 3 1/8"

2. 9/64 = .140625 = .1406

3. 1'2 3/16" + 1'5 1/2" + 1'4 5/8" = 3'11 21/16" = 4'5/16"

4. 3 5/16" ÷ 1/8" = 53/16 × 8/1 = 26.5. Then, (26.5)(1 ft.) = 26.5 feet

5. 50,631 - 39,842 = 10,789; 10,789 ÷ 100 = 107.89
   Since the cost is .23 per 100 cubic feet or any fraction thereof, the cost will be
   (.23)(107) + .23 = $24.84

6. 9740 ÷ 1.04 = 9365 cu.ft.

7. 40 ÷ 7.5 = 5 1/3 cu.ft. of water per minute. The volume = (6)(5)(4) = 120 cu.ft. Thus, the number of minutes needed to fill the tank is 120 ÷ 5 1/3 = 22.5

8. 3" pipe: 3 × 7'6" = 22 1/2' × 14.5 lbs. = 326.25
   4" pipe: 4 × 5' = 20' × 13 lbs. = 260
   326.25 + 260 = 586.25 (most nearly 585)

9. Let x = pressure. Then, 34/12 = 14.7/x. So, 34x = 176.4
   Solving, x ≈ 5 lbs./sq.in.

10. (8)(9)(63) = 4536 cu.ft. Since 1 cu.yd. = 27 cu.ft., 4536 cu.ft. is equivalent to 168 cu.yds.

11. Let x = correct amount. Then, $\dfrac{1}{1200} = \dfrac{1\frac{1}{3}}{x}$. Solving, x = 1600

12. 87,463 - 17,377 = 70,086; and 70,086 ÷ 100 = 700.86 ≈ 700 Then, (700)(.15) = $105.00

13. Cross-sectional area of a 6" diameter pipe = $(\pi)(3")^2 = 9\pi$ sq. in. Note that the combined cross-sectional areas of four 3" diameter pipes = $(4)(\pi)(1.5")^2 = 9\pi$ sq. in.

14. 90 - 50 = 40 gals/min. Then, 2950 ÷ 40 = 73.75 min. ≈ 1 hr. 14 min.

15. Volume = $(\pi)(4)^2(3\,1/2) = 56\pi$ cu.ft. Then, $(56\pi)(7.5)$ = 1320 gals.

16. For 4100 cu.ft., the charge of (.525)(41) = $21,525 > $21

17. Rent = $73,500 + (5)($52.50) = $997,50. For demolition, the charge = (3/8)($997.50) $374

18. (1/4")(7.75) = 2"

19. (3")(8) = 24" = 2 ft.

20. Let x = weight. Then, 500/800 = 120/x . Solving, x = 192 190 lbs.

21. (3')(5 1/2')(50') = 825 cu.ft. Then, 825 ÷ 27 ≈ 30 cu.yds.

22. Net pay = (.82)($86,500) = $70,930/yr. Weekly pay = $70,930 ÷ 52 ≈ $1365

23. (12x3) + (12x4) +24+4+6+2= 120

24. The shortest side = (1/2)(hypotenuse) = (1/2)(12') = 6'

25. 2'6 1/4" + 3'9 3/8" + 4'7 5/8" + 5'8 7/8 " = 14'30 17/8" = 16'8 1/8"

TEST 2

DIRECTIONS: Each question or incomplete statement is followed by several suggested answers or completions. Select the one that BEST answers the question or completes the statement. *PRINT THE LETTER OF THE CORRECT ANSWER IN THE SPACE AT THE RIGHT.*

1. The sum of the following pipe lengths, 15 5/8", 8 3/4", 30 5/16" and 20 1/2", is   1.____

   A. 77 1/8"   B. 76 3/16"   C. 75 3/16"   D. 74 5/16"

2. If the outside diameter of a pipe is 6 inches and the wall thickness is 1/2 inch, the inside area of this pipe, in square inches, is MOST NEARLY   2.____

   A. 15.7   B. 17.3   C. 19.6   D. 23.8

3. Three lengths of pipe 1'10", 3'2 1/2", and 5'7 1/2", respectively, are to be cut from a pipe 14'0" long.
Allowing 1/8" for each pipe cut, the length of pipe remaining is   3.____

   A. 3'1 1/8"   B. 3'2 1/2"   C. 3'3 1/4"   D. 3'3 5/8"

4. According to the building code, the MAXIMUM permitted surface temperature of combustible construction materials located near heating equipment is 76.5°C. (°F=(°Cx9/5)+32) Maximum temperature Fahrenheit is MOST NEARLY   4.____

   A. 170° F   B. 195° F   C. 210° F   D. 220° F

5. A pump discharges 7.5 gals/minutes.
In 2.5 hours the pump will discharge _____ gallons.   5.____

   A. 1125   B. 1875   C. 1950   D. 2200

6. A pipe with an outside diameter of 4" has a circumference of MOST NEARLY _____ inches.   6.____

   A. 8.05   B. 9.81   C. 12.57   D. 14.92

7. A piping sketch is drawn to a scale of 1/8" = 1 foot.
A vertical steam line measuring 3 1/2" on the sketch would have an ACTUAL length of _____ feet.   7.____

   A. 16   B. 22   C. 24   D. 28

8. A pipe having an inside diameter of 3.48 inches and a wall thickness of .18 inches will have an outside diameter of _____ inches.   8.____

   A. 3.84   B. 3.64   C. 3.57   D. 3.51

9. A rectangular steel bar having a volume of 30 cubic inches, a width of 2 inches, and a height of 3 inches will have a length of _____ inches.   9.____

   A. 12   B. 10   C. 8   D. 5

10. A pipe weighs 20.4 pounds per foot of length.
The total weight of eight pieces of this pipe with each piece 20 feet in length is MOST NEARLY _____ pounds.   10.____

    A. 460   B. 1,680   C. 2,420   D. 3,260

11. Assume that four pieces of pipe measuring 2'1 1/4", 4'2 3/4", 5'1 9/16", and 6'3 5/8", respectively, are cut with a saw from a pipe 20"0" long.
Allowing 1/16" waste for each cut, the length of the remaining pipe is

    A. 2'1 9/16"   B. 2'2 9/16"   C. 2'4 13/16"   D. 2'8 9/16"

12. If one cubic inch of steel weighs 0.28 pounds, the weight, in pounds, of a steel bar 1/2" x 6" x 2'0" long is MOST NEARLY

    A. 11   B. 16   C. 20   D. 24

13. If the circumference of a circle is equal to 31.416 inches, then its diameter, in inches, is equal to MOST NEARLY

    A. 8   B. 9   C. 10   D. 13

14. Assume that a steam fitter's helper receives a salary of $171.36 a day for 250 days is considered a full work year. If taxes, social security, hospitalization, and pension deducted from his salary amounts to 16 percent of his gross pay, then his net yearly salary will be MOST NEARLY

    A. $31,788   B. $35,982   C. $41,982   D. $42,840

15. If the outside diameter of a pipe is 14 inches and the wall thickness is 1/2 inch, then the inside area of the pipe, in square inches, is MOST NEARLY

    A. 125   B. 133   C. 143   D. 154

16. A steam leak in a pipe line allows steam to escape at a rate of 50,000 pounds each month.
Assuming that the cost of steam is $2.50 per 1,000 pounds, the TOTAL cost of wasted steam from this leak for a 12-month period would amount to

    A. $125   B. $300   C. $1,500   D. $3,000

17. If 250 feet of 4" pipe weighs 400 pounds, the weight of this pipe per linear foot is _____ pounds.

    A. 1.25   B. 1.50   C. 1.60   D. 1.75

18. A set of heating plan drawings is drawn to a scale of 1/4" = 1 foot.
If a length of pipe measures 4 5/8" on the drawing, the ACTUAL length of the pipe, in feet, is

    A. 16.3   B. 16.8   C. 17.5   D. 18.5

19. The TOTAL length of four pieces of pipe whose lengths are 3'4 1/2", 2'1 5/16", 4'9 3/8", and 2'3 1/4", respectively, is

    A. 11'5 7/16"   B. 11'6 7/16"
    C. 12'5 7/16"   D. 12'6 7/16"

20. Assume that a pipe trench is 3 feet wide, 3 feet deep, and 300 feet long.
If the unit cost of excavating the trench is $120 per cubic yard, the TOTAL cost of excavating the trench is

    A. $1,200   B. $12,000   C. $27,000   D. $36,000

21. The TOTAL length of four pieces of 1 1/2" galvanized steel pipe whose lengths are 7 ft. + 3 1/2 inches, 4 ft. + 2 1/4 inches, 6 ft. + 7 inches, and 8 ft. +5 1/8 inches is   21._____

    A. 26 feet + 5 7/8 inches
    B. 25 ft. + 6 7/8 inches
    C. 25 feet + 4 1/4 inches
    D. 25 ft. + 3 3/8 inches

22. A swimming pool is 25' wide by 75' long and has an average depth of 5'. 1 cubic foot contains 7.5 gallons of water. The capacity, when filled to the overflow, is _____ gallons.   22._____

    A. 9,375   B. 65,625   C. 69,005   D. 70,312

23. The sum of 3 1/4, 5 1/8, 2 1/2 , and 3 3/8 is   23._____

    A. 14   B. 14 1/8   C. 14 1/4   D. 14 3/8

24. Assume that it takes 6 men 8 days to do a particular job. If you have only 4 men available to do this job and they all work at the same speed, then the number of days it would take to complete the job would be   24._____

    A. 11   B. 12   C. 13   D. 14

25. The total length of four pieces of 2" O.D. pipe, whose lengths are 7'3 1/2", 4'2 3/16", 5'7 5/16", and 8'5 7/8", respectively, is MOST NEARLY   25._____

    A. 24'6 3/4"
    B. 24'7 15/16"
    C. 25'5 13/16"
    D. 25'6 7/8"

KEY (CORRECT ANSWERS)

1.	C	11.	B
2.	C	12.	C
3.	D	13.	C
4.	A	14.	B
5.	A	15.	B
6.	C	16.	C
7.	D	17.	C
8.	A	18.	D
9.	D	19.	D
10.	D	20.	B

21. A
22. D
23. C
24. B
25. D

SOLUTIONS TO PROBLEMS

1. 15 5/8" + 8 3/4" + 30 5/16" + 20 1/2" = 73 35/16" = 75 3/16"

2. Inside diameter = 6" - 1/2" - 1/2" = 5". Area = (π)(5/2")^2 ≈ 19.6 sq. in.

3. Pipe remaining = 14' - 1'10" - 3'2 1/2" - 5'7 1/2" - (3)(1/8") = 3'3 5/8"

4. 76.5 x 9/5 = 137.7 + 32 = 169.7

5. 7.5 x 150 = 1125

6. Radius = 2" Circumference = (2π)(2") ≈ 12.57"

7. 3 1/2" 1/8" = (7/2)(8/1) = 28 Then, (28)(1 ft.) = 28 feet

8. Outside diameter = 3.48" + .18" + .18" = 3.84"

9. 30 = (2)(3)(length). So, length = 5"

10. Total weight = (20.4)(8)(20) ≈ 3260 lbs.

11. 20' - 2'1 1/4" - 4'2 3/4" - 5'1 9/16" - 6'3 5/8" - (4)(1/16") = 2'2 9/16"

12. Weight = (.28)(1/2")(6")(24") = 20.16 ≈ 20 lbs.

13. Diameter = 31.416" ÷ π ≈ 10"

14. His net pay for 250 days = (.84)($171.36)(250) = $35,985.60 ≈ $35,928 (from answer key)

15. Inside diameter = 14" - 1/2" - 1/2" = 13". Area = (π)(13/2")^2 ≈ 133 sq.in

16. (50,000 lbs.)(12) = 600,000 lbs. per year. The cost would be ($2.50)(600) = $1500

17. 400 ÷ 250 = 1.60 pounds per linear foot

18. 4 5/8" ÷ 1/4" = 37/8 . 4/1 = 18.5 Then, (18.5)(1 ft.) = 18.5 feet

19. 3'4 1/2" + 2'1 5/16" + 4'9 3/8" + 2'3 1/4" = 11'17 23/16" = 12'6 7/16"

20. (3')(3')(300') = 2700 cu.ft., which is 2700 ÷ 27 = 100 cu.yds. Total cost = ($120)(100) = $12,000

21. 7'3 1/2" + 4'2 1/4" + 6'7" + 8'5 1/8" = 25'17 7/8" = 26'5 7/8"

22. (25)(75)(5) = 9375 cu.ft. Then, (9375)(7.5) ≈ 70,312 gals.

23. 3 1/4 + 5 1/8 + 2 1/2 + 3 3/8 = 13 10/8 = 14 1/4

24. (6) (8) = 48 man-days. Then, 48 ÷ 4 = 12 days

25. 7'3 1/2" + 4'2 3/16" + 5'7 5/16" + 8'5 7/8" = 24'17 30/16" = 25'6 7/8"

TEST 3

DIRECTIONS: Each question or incomplete statement is followed by several suggested answers or completions. Select the one that BEST answers the question or completes the statement. *PRINT THE LETTER OF THE CORRECT ANSWER IN THE SPACE AT THE RIGHT.*

1. The time required to pump 2,500 gallons of water out of a sump at the rate of 12 1/2 gallons per minutes would be _____ hour(s) _____ minutes.

    A. 1; 40 B. 2; 30 C. 3; 20 D. 6; 40

2. Copper tubing which has an inside diameter of 1 1/16" and a wall thickness of .095" has an outside diameter which is MOST NEARLY _____ inches.

    A. 1 5/32 B. 1 3/16 C. 1 7/32 D. 1 1/4

3. Assume that 90 gallons per minute flow through a certain 3-inch pipe which is tapped into a street main.
    The amount of water which would flow through a 1-inch pipe tapped into the same street main is MOST NEARLY _____ gpm.

    A. 90 B. 45 C. 30 D. 10

4. The weight of a 6 foot length of 8-inch pipe which weighs 24.70 pounds per foot is _____ lbs.

    A. 148.2 B. 176.8 C. 197.6 D. 212.4

5. If a 4-inch pipe is directly coupled to a 2-inch pipe and 16 gallons per minute are flowing through the 4-inch pipe, then the flow through the 2-inch pipe will be _____ gallons per minute.

    A. 4 B. 8 C. 16 D. 32

6. If the water pressure at the bottom of a column of water 34 feet high is 14.7 pounds per square inch, the water pressure at the bottom of a column of water 18 feet high is MOST NEARLY _____ pounds per square inch.

    A. 8.0 B. 7.8 C. 7.6 D. 7.4

7. If there are 7 1/2 gallons in a cubic foot of water and if water flows from a hose at a constant rate of 4 gallons per minute, the time it should take to COMPLETELY fill a tank of 1,600 cubic feet capacity with water from that hose is _____ hours.

    A. 300 B. 150 C. 100 D. 50

8. Each of a group of fifteen water meter readers read an average of 62 water meters a day in a certain 5-day work week. A total of 5,115 meters are read by this group the following week.
    The TOTAL number of meters read in the second week as compared to the first week shows a

    A. 10% increase B. 15% increase
    C. 20% increase D. 5% decrease

9. A certain water consumer used 5% more water in 1994 than he did in 1993. If his water consumption for 1994 was 8,375 cubic feet, the amount of water he consumed in 1993 was MOST NEARLY _____ cubic feet.

   A. 9,014   B. 8,816   C. 7,976   D. 6,776

10. Assume that a water meter reads 40,175 cubic feet and that the previous reading was 29,186 cubic feet.
    If the charge for water is 92 cents per 100 cubic feet or any fraction thereof, the bill for the amount of water used since the previous meter reading should be

    A. $100.28   B. $101.04   C. $101.08   D. $101.20

11. A leaking faucet caused a loss of 216 cubic feet of water in a 30-day month. If there are 7.5 gallons in a cubic foot of water, then the AVERAGE loss of water per hour for that month was _____ gallons.

    A. 2 1/4   B. 2 1/8   C. 2   D. 1 3/4

12. The fraction which is equal to .375 is

    A. 3/16   B. 5/32   C. 3/8   D. 5/12

13. A square backyard swimming pool, each side of which is 10 feet long, is filled to a depth of 3 1/2 feet.
    If there are 7 1/2 gallons in a cubic foot of water, the number of gallons of water in the pool is MOST NEARLY _____ gallons.

    A. 46.7   B. 100   C. 2,625   D. 3,500

14. When 1 5/8, 3 3/4, 6 1/3, and 9 1/2 are added, the resulting sum is

    A. 21 1/8   B. 21 1/6   C. 21 5/24   D. 21 1/4

15. When 946 1/2 is subtracted from 1,035 1/4, the result is

    A. 87 1/4   B. 87 3/4   C. 88 1/4   D. 88 3/4

16. When 39 is multiplied by 697, the result is

    A. 8,364   B. 26,283   C. 27,183   D. 28,003

17. When 16.074 is divided by .045, the result is

    A. 3.6   B. 35.7   C. 357.2   D. 3,572

18. To dig a trench 3'0" wide, 50'0" long, and 5'6" deep, the total number of cubic yards of earth to be removed is MOST NEARLY

    A. 30   B. 90   C. 140   D. 825

19. The TOTAL length of four pieces of 2" pipe, whose lengths are 7'3 1/2", 4'2 3/16", 5'7 5/16", and 8'5 7/8", respectively, is

    A. 24'6 3/4"   B. 24'7 15/16"
    C. 25'5 13/16"   D. 25'6 7/8"

20. A hot water line made of copper has a straight horizontal run of 150 feet and, when installed, is at a temperature of 45° F. In use, its temperature rises to 190° F.
    If the coefficient of expansion for copper is 0.0000095" per foot per degree F, the TOTAL expansion, in inches, in the run of pipe is given by the product of 150 multiplied by 0.0000095 by

    A. 145
    B. 145 x 12
    C. 145 divided by 12
    D. 145 x 12 x 12

21. A water storage tank measures 5' long, 4' wide, and 6' deep and is filled to the 5 1/2' mark with water.
    If one cubic foot of water weighs 62 pounds, the number of pounds of water required to COMPLETELY fill the tank is

    A. 7,440   B. 6,200   C. 1,240   D. 620

22. Assume that a pipe worker earns $83,125.00 per year.
    If seventeen percent of his pay is deducted for taxes, social security, and pension, his net weekly pay will be APPROXIMATELY

    A. $1598.50   B. $1504.00   C. $1453.00   D. $1325.00

23. If eighteen feet of 4" cast iron pipe weighs approximately 390 pounds, the weight of this pipe per lineal foot will be MOST NEARLY _____ lbs.

    A. 19   B. 22   C. 23   D. 25

24. If it takes 3 men 11 days to dig a trench, the number of days it will take 5 men to dig the same trench, assuming all work is done at the same rate of speed, is MOST NEARLY

    A. 6 1/2   B. 7 3/4   C. 8 1/4   D. 8 3/4

25. If a trench is dug 6'0" deep, 2'6" wide, and 8'0" long, the area of the opening, in square feet, is MOST NEARLY

    A. 48   B. 32   C. 20   D. 15

KEY (CORRECT ANSWERS)

1.	C	11.	A
2.	D	12.	C
3.	D	13.	C
4.	A	14.	C
5.	B	15.	D
6.	B	16.	C
7.	D	17.	C
8.	A	18.	A
9.	C	19.	D
10.	D	20.	A

21. D
22. D
23. B
24. A
25. C

SOLUTIONS TO PROBLEMS

1. 2500 ÷ 12 1/2 = 200 min. = 3 hrs. 20 min.

2. 1 1/16" + .095" + .095" = 1.0625 + .095 + .095 = 1.2525" ≈ 1 1/4"

3. Cross-sectional areas for a 3-inch pipe and a 1-inch pipe are $(\pi)(1.5)^2$ and $(\pi)(.5)^2$ = 2.25 π and .25 π, respectively. Let x = amount of water flowing through the 1-inch pipe. Then, $\frac{90}{x} = \frac{2.25\pi}{.25\pi}$. Solving, x = 10 gals/min

4. (24.70)(6) = 148.2 lbs.

5. $\frac{4" \text{ pipe}}{16 \text{ gallons}} = \frac{2" \text{ pipe}}{x \text{ gallons}}$, 4x = 32, x = 8

6. Let x = pressure. Then, 34/18 = 14.7/x. Solving, x ≈ 7.8

7. (1600)(7.5) = 12,000 gallons. Then, 12,000 ÷ 4 = 3000 min. = 50 hours

8. (15)(62)(5) = 4650. Then, (5115-4650)/4650 = 10% increase

9. 8375 ÷ 1.05 ≈ 7976 cu.ft.

10. 40,175 - 29,186 = 10,989 cu.ft. Then, 10,989 100 = 109.89. Since .92 is charged for each 100 cu.ft. or fraction thereof, total cost = (.92)(110) = $101.20

11. (216)(7.5) = 1620 gallons. In 30 days, there are 720 hours. Thus, the average water loss per hour = 1620 ÷ 720 = 2 1/4 gallons.

12. .375 = 375/1000 = 3/8

13. Volume = (10)(10)(3 1/2) = 350 cu.ft. Then, (350)(7 1/2) = 2625 gallons

14. 1 5/8 + 3 3/4 + 6 1/3 + 9 1/2 = 19 53/24 = 21 5/24

15. 1035 1/4 - 946 1/2 = 88 3/4

16. (39)(697) = 27,183

17. 16.074 .045 = 357.2

18. (3')(50')(5 1/2') = 825 cu.ft. ≈ 30 cu.yds., since 1 cu.yd. = 27 cu.ft.

19. 7'3 1/2" + 4'2 3/16" + 5'7 5/16" + 8'5 7/8" = 24'17 30/16" = 25'6 7/8"

20. Total expansion = (150)(.0000095)(145)

21. Number of pounds needed = (5) (4)(6-5 1/2)(62) = 620

22. Net annual pay = ($83,125)(.83) ≈ $69000. Then, the net weekly pay = $69000 ÷ 52 ≈ $1325 (actually about $1327)

23. 390 lbs. ÷ 18 = 21.6 lbs. per linear foot

24. (3)(11) = 33 man-days. Then, 33 ÷ 5 = 6.6 ≈ 6 1/2 days

25. Area = (8')(2 1/2') = 20 sq.ft.

BASIC FUNDAMENTALS OF BOILERS

TABLE OF CONTENTS

		Page
I.	NATURE	1
II.	CLASSIFICATION	2
	A. Location of Fire and Water Spaces	2
	B. Size of Tubes	2
	C. Type of Circulation	2
	D. Type of Superheat	3
III.	TERMINOLOGY	3
	A. Fire Room and Boiler Room	4
	B. Boiler Emergency Station	4
	C. Boiler Full-Power Capacity	4
	D. Boiler Overload Capacity	4
	E. Superheater Outlet Pressure	4
	F. Steam Drum Pressure	4
	G. Design Pressure	4
	H. Operating Pressure	4
	I. Boiler Efficiency	4
	J. Fire Room Efficiency	4
	K. Total Heating Surface	5
	L. Generating Surface	5
	M. Superheater Surface	5
	N. Economizer Surface	5
	O. Steaming Hours	5

BASIC FUNDAMENTALS OF BOILERS

I. NATURE

The boiler is the source or high-temperature region of the thermos-dynamic cycle. The steam that is generated in the boiler is led to the turbines, where its thermal energy is converted into mechanical energy (work) which drives the unit and provides power for vital services.

In essence, a boiler is merely a container in which water can be boiled and steam generated. A tea kettle on a stove is basically a boiler, although a rather inefficient one. Note that the steam is generated in one vessel and superheated in another, since it is impossible to raise the temperature of the steam above the temperature of the boiling water as long as the two are in contact with each other.

In designing a boiler which must produce a large amount of steam, it is obviously necessary to find some means of providing a larger amount of heat-transfer surface than could be provided by a vessel shaped like a tea kettle. In most modern boilers, the steam generating surface consists of hundreds and hundreds of tubes, which provide a maximum amount of heat-transfer surface in a relatively small space. As a rule, the tubes communicate with a steam drum at the top of a boiler and with water drums and headers at the bottom of the boiler. The tubes and part of the drums are enclosed in an insulated capsule which has space inside it for the furnace. A boiler appears to be a fairly complicated piece of equipment when it is considered with all its fittings, piping, and accessories; it may be helpful, therefore, to remember that the basic components of a saturated-steam boiler are merely the tubes, the drums, and headers, and the furnace.

Practically all boilers used in propulsion are designed to produce both saturated steam and superheated steam. To our basic boiler, therefore, we must now add another component: the superheater. The superheater on most boilers consist of headers, usually located at the back of the boiler, and a number of superheater tubes which communicate with the headers. Saturated steam from the steam drum is led through the superheater; since the steam is now no longer in contact with the water from which it was generated, the steam becomes superheated as additional heat is supplied. In some boilers, there is a separate superheater furnace; in others, the superheater tubes project into the same furnace that is used for the generation of saturated steam.

Some question may arise concerning the need for both saturated steam and superheated steam. Saturated steam is used for operating most steam-driven auxiliary machinery; reciprocating machinery, in particular, requires saturated steam for the lubrication of the moving parts of the steam end. Superheated steam is used almost exclusively for the propulsion turbines. There is more available energy in superheated steam than in saturated steam at the same pressure; and the use of higher temperatures vastly increases the efficiency of the propulsion cycle since, as we have seen, the efficiency of a heat engine is dependent upon the absolute temperature at the source (boiler) and the absolute temperature at the receiver (condenser). In some instances, the gain in efficiency resulting from the use of superheated steam may be as much as 15 percent for 200 degrees of superheat. This increase in efficiency is particularly important because it allows substantial savings in fuel consumption and in space and weight requirements. A further advantage in using superheated steam for propulsion machinery is that it causes relatively little erosion since it is free of moisture

II. CLASSIFICATION

Boilers may be classified in a number of different ways, according to various design features. Most commonly, they are classified and described in terms of (1) the relative location of the fire and water spaces, (2) the size of the tubes, (3) the type of circulation, and (4) the type of superheat. Some knowledge of these methods of classification will be useful in understanding the design and construction of modern boilers.

A. Location of Fire and Water Spaces

First of all, boilers are classified according to the relative location of their fire and water spaces. By this classification, all boilers may be divided into two groups: *fire-tube boilers* and *water-tube boilers*. In *fire-tube boilers*, the gases of combustion flow through the tubes and thereby heat the surrounding water. In *water-tube boilers*, the water flows through the tubes and is heated by the gases of combustion that fill the furnace.

B. Size of Tubes

Water-tube boilers are further classified according to the size of the tubes. Boilers having tubes 2 inches or more in diameter are called *large-tube boilers*. Boilers having tubes less than 2 inches in diameter are called *small-tube* or *express-type boilers*.

C. Type of Circulation

Water-tube boilers are also classified as *natural circulation boilers* or as *force circulation boilers*, depending upon the way in which the water circulates within the boiler.

Natural circulation boilers are those in which the circulation of water depends upon the difference in density between an ascending mixture of hot water and steam and a descending body of relatively cool and steam-free water. Natural circulation may be of two types, free or accelerated.

In this type of boiler, the generating tubes are installed at a slight angle of inclination which allows the lighter hot water and steam to rise while the cooler (and heavier) water descends.

Installing the generating tubes at a greater angle of inclination increases the rate of water circulation. Hence, boilers in which the tubes slope more steeply are said to have accelerated natural circulation.

Most modern boilers are designed for accelerated natural circulation. In such boilers, large tubes (3 or more inches in diameter) are installed between the steam drum and the water drums. These tubes, called *downcomers*, are located outside the furnace and away from the heat of combustion, thereby serving as pathways for the downward flow of relatively cool water. When a sufficient number of downcomers are installed, all small tubes can be generating tubes, carrying steam and water upward; and all downward flow can be carried by the downcomer. The size and number of downcomers installed varies from one type of boiler to another.

Forced circulation boilers are, as their name implies, quite different in design from the boilers that utilize natural circulation. Instead of depending upon differences in density between the hotter and the cooler water, forced circulation boilers use pumps to force the water through the various boiler circuits. Forced circulation boilers are relatively new, but they have some very definite advantages which will probably lead to their increased use in the future.

   D. Type of Superheat

Practically all boilers are equipped with superheaters. With respect to the superheater installation, boilers are classified as having either controlled superheat or uncontrolled superheat. In a boiler with *controlled superheat*, the degree of superheat can be changed by regulating the amount of heat supplied to the superheater tube bank, without substantially changing the amount of heat supplied to the generating tubes. This control of superheat is possible because the boiler has two furnaces, one for the saturated side and one for the superheat side. A boiler with *uncontrolled superheat*, on the other hand, has only one furnace; and since the same furnace must be used for heating both the generating tubes and the superheater tubes, the degree of superheat cannot be controlled but varies within a small range as a function of design and firing rate.

Various terms are used to describe these two basic types of superheaters. Where the superheat is controlled, the superheater is often referred to as an *integral, separately fired superheat*, and the boiler as a whole is called a *superheat control boiler*. Where the superheat is not controlled, the superheater may be called an *integral, not separately fired superheater*, or it may be referred to as a *no control,* or *uncontrolled superheater,* and the boiler as a whole is called a *no control* or *uncontrolled superheat boiler*. The term *integral* is used to indicate that the superheater is installed as a part of the boiler unit. Practically all superheaters on modern boilers are integral with the boilers.

On both controlled and uncontrolled superheat boilers, the superheater tubes are protected from radiant heat by generation tubes that are called *water screen tubes*. The water screen tubes absorb the intense radiant heat of the furnace, and the superheater tubes are heated by convection currents rather than by direct radiation. Hence, the superheaters are sometimes called *convection-type superheaters.*

Some older types of superheat control boilers had *radiant-type superheaters*—that is, the superheater tubes were not screened by water tubes but were exposed directly to the radiant heat of the furnace. However, this type of superheater is relatively uncommon at the present time and will, therefore, not be further discussed.

III. TERMINOLOGY

In order to ensure uniform use of terms, there has been established a number of standard terms and definitions pertaining to boilers. Some of the more important of these definitions are given below.

A. Fire Room and Boiler Room: A compartment which contains boilers and the station for operating them is called a *fire room*. A compartment which contains boilers which does not contain the station for operating them is called a *boiler room*.

B. Boiler Emergency Station: This term is used to designate a station which is so located that, in the event of trouble, one may proceed with minimum delay to any fire room, boiler operating station, or boiler room.

C. Boiler Full-Power Capacity: The total quantity of steam required to develop contract shaft horsepower of the vessel, divided by the number of boilers installed, gives boiler full-power capacity. The quantity of steam is given in pounds of water evaporated per hour. Full-power capacity is indicated in the manufacturer's technical manual for each boiler.

D. Boiler Overload Capacity: Boiler overload capacity is specified in the design of the boiler. It is given in terms of steaming rate or firing rate, depending upon the individual installation. Boiler overload capacity is usually 120 percent of boiler full-power capacity.

E. Superheater Outlet Pressure: This is the actual steam pressure at the superheater outlet.

F. Steam Drum Pressure: This is the pressure in the steam drum. Steam drum pressure is specified in the design of a boiler and is given in the manufacturer's technical manual for each boiler. Steam drum pressure is the pressure which must be carried in the boiler steam drum in order to obtain the required pressure at the turbine throttles, when steaming at full-power capacity. Ordinarily, the designed steam drum pressure is carried for all steaming conditions.

G. Design Pressure: Design pressure is the pressure specified by the boiler manufacturer as a criterion for boiler design. It is usually 103 percent of steam drum pressure.

H. Operating Pressure: Operating pressure is the pressure at the final outlet from a boiler, after steam has passed through all baffles, the dry pipe, the superheater, etc., when the boiler is steaming at full-power capacity. Operating pressure is specified in the design of a boiler and is given in the manufacturer's technical manual. Operating pressure is the same as superheater outlet pressure when the boiler is steaming at full-power capacity; when the boiler is steaming at less than full-power capacity, however, the actual pressure at the superheater outlet will vary from the specified operating pressure provided a constant drum pressure is maintained.

I. Boiler Efficiency: The efficiency of a boiler is the British thermal units per pound of fuel absorbed by the water and steam divided by the British thermal units per pound of fuel fired. In other words, boiler efficiency is output divided by input, or Btu utilized divided by Btu available. Boiler efficiency is expressed as a percentage.

J. Fire Room Efficiency: The boiler efficiency corrected for blower and pump steam consumption is known as fire room efficiency. (This is not the same as boiler plant efficiency or propulsion plant efficiency.)

K. Total Heating Surface: The total heating surface of any steam generating unit consists of that portion of the heat transfer apparatus which is exposed on one side to the gases of combustion and on the other side to the water or steam being heated. Thus, the total heating surface equals the sum of the generating surface, the superheater surface, and the economizer surface. All heating surfaces are measured on the combustion-gas side.

L. Generating Surface: The generating surface is that portion of the total heating surface in which the fluid being heated forms part of the circulating system. The generating surface includes the boiler tube banks, water walls, water screens, and water floors (where installed and not covered by refractory material.)

M. Superheater Surface: The superheater surface is that portion of the total heating surface where the steam is heated after leaving the boiler steam drum.

N. Economizer Surface: The economizer surface is that portion of the total heating surface where the feed water is heated before entering the generating system.

O. Steaming Hours: The term steaming hours includes the time during which the boiler has fires lighted for raising steam and the time during which it is generating steam. Time during which fires are not lighted is not included in steaming hours.

www.ingramcontent.com/pod-product-compliance
Lightning Source LLC
Chambersburg PA
CBHW081831300426
44116CB00014B/2543